2018 SQA Specimen and Past Papers with Answers

Higher
BIOLOGY

2017 & 2018 Exams
and 2018 Specimen Question Paper

HODDER
GIBSON
AN HACHETTE UK COMPANY

This book contains the official SQA 2017 and 2018 Exams, and the 2018 Specimen Question Paper for Higher Biology, with associated SQA-approved answers modified from the official marking instructions that accompany the paper.

In addition the book contains study skills advice. This advice has been specially commissioned by Hodder Gibson, and has been written by experienced senior teachers and examiners in line with the Higher syllabus and assessment outlines. This is not SQA material but has been devised to provide further guidance for Higher examinations.

Hachette UK's policy is to use papers that are natural, renewable and recyclable products and made from wood grown in sustainable forests. The logging and manufacturing processes are expected to conform to the environmental regulations of the country of origin.

Orders: please contact Bookpoint Ltd, 130 Park Drive, Milton Park, Abingdon, Oxon OX14 4SE. Telephone: (44) 01235 827827. Fax: (44) 01235 400454. Lines are open 9.00–5.00, Monday to Saturday, with a 24-hour message answering service. Visit our website at www.hoddereducation.co.uk. Hodder Gibson can also be contacted directly at hoddergibson@hodder.co.uk

This collection first published in 2018 by
Hodder Gibson, an imprint of Hodder Education,
An Hachette UK Company
211 St Vincent Street
Glasgow G2 5QY

Typeset by Aptara, Inc.

Printed in the UK

A catalogue record for this title is available from the British Library

ISBN: 978-1-5104-5669-3

2 1

2019 2018

Introduction

Higher Biology

The practice papers in this book give you an overall and comprehensive coverage of assessment of **Knowledge** and **Scientific Inquiry** for Higher Biology.

We recommend that you download and print a copy of Higher Biology Assessment Specification pages 33–75 from the SQA website at www.sqa.org.uk/sqa/47912.html This document tells you what will be tested in your examination. You should note that both the Key Area and Depth of Knowledge columns can be examined.

It is expected that you be familiar with the apparatus and techniques detailed on page 75.

The course

The Higher Biology Course consists of three Areas of Biology. These are DNA and the Genome, Metabolism and Survival and Sustainability and Interdependence. In each Area you will be assessed on your ability to demonstrate and apply knowledge of Biology and to demonstrate and apply skills of scientific inquiry. Candidates must also complete an Assignment in which they research a topic in biology and write it up as a report. They also take a Course examination.

How the course is graded

The grade you achieve for Higher Biology depends on the following two course assessments, which are set and graded by SQA.

1. A report based on an Assignment, which is worth 20% of the grade. The Assignment is marked out of 20 marks, which is then scaled to 30 marks.

2. A written course examination is worth the remaining 80% of the grade. The examination is marked out of 120 marks, most of which are for the demonstration and application of knowledge although there are also marks available for skills of scientific inquiry.

This book should help you practise the examination part! To pass Higher Biology with a C grade you will need about 50% of the 150 marks available for the Assignment and the Course Examination combined. For a B you will need roughly 60% and, for an A, roughly 70%.

The course examination

The Course Examination consists of two Papers.

- Paper 1 is an objective test with 25 multiple-choice items for 25 marks.
- Paper 2 is a mix of restricted and extended-response questions worth between 1 and 10 marks each for a total of 95 marks. The majority of the marks test knowledge with an emphasis on the application of knowledge. The remainder, test the application of scientific inquiry, analysis and problem solving skills. There will always be a large experimental question and a large data handling question worth between 5 and 9 marks each. There will be two or three extended-response questions worth between 10 and 15 marks in total. At least one of the extended-response questions will include a choice of topic.

Altogether, there are 120 marks and you will have 40 minutes to complete Paper 1, a 30 minute break followed by 2 hours and 20 minutes to complete Paper 2. The majority of the marks will be straightforward and linked to grade C but about 30% of the marks are more demanding and are linked to grade A.

General tips and hints

Each paper in this book can be attempted in its entirety or groups of questions on a particular topic or skill area can be attempted. If you are trying a whole examination paper from this book, give yourself 2 hours and 30 minutes maximum to complete either the 2017 or 2018 Papers, and allow 3 hours for the Specimen Paper. Make sure that you spend time in using the answer section to mark your own work – it is especially useful if you can get someone to help you with this.

The marking instructions give acceptable answers with alternatives. You could even grade your work on an A–D basis. The following hints and tips are related to examination techniques as well as avoiding common mistakes. Remember that if you hit problems with a question, you should ask your teacher for help.

Paper 1

25 multiple-choice items **25 marks**

- Answer on a grid.
- You are allocated 40 minutes to complete this Paper.
- Some individual questions might take longer to answer than others – this is quite normal and make sure you use scrap paper if a calculation or any working is needed.
- Some questions can be answered instantly – again, this is normal.
- Do not leave blanks – complete the grid for each question as you work through.
- Try to answer each question in your head without looking at the options. If your answer is there you are home and dry!
- If you are not certain, choose the answer that seemed most attractive on first reading the answer options.
- If you are guessing, try to eliminate options before making your guess. If you can eliminate three – you are left with the correct answer even if you do not recognise it!

Paper 2

Restricted and extended-response questions **95 marks**

- You are allocated 2 hours and 20 minutes for this Paper.
- Answer on the question paper. Try to write neatly and keep your answers on the support lines if possible – the lines are designed to take the full answer!
- A clue to answer length is the mark allocation – most questions are restricted to 1 mark and the answer can be quite short. If there are 2–4 marks available, your answer will need to be extended and may well have two, three or even four parts. A rough guide to timing is 1.5 minutes per mark but this can vary.
- Questions are designed to test the content within a key area but some questions are integrated and may contain content from more than one key area.
- The C-type questions usually start with "State", "Identify", "Give" or "Name" and often need only a word or two in response. They will usually be for 1 mark each.
- Questions that begin with "Explain", "Describe" or "Suggest" are usually A-types and are likely to have more than one part to the full answer. You will usually have to write a sentence or two and there may be 2 or even 3 marks available.
- Make sure you read questions over twice before trying to answer – there is often very important information within the question and you are unlikely to be short of time in this examination.

- Using abbreviations like DNA and ATP is fine and the bases of DNA can be given as A, T, G and C. The Higher Biology Course Specification will give you the acceptable abbreviations.
- Don't worry that a few questions are in unfamiliar contexts, that's the idea! Just keep calm and read the questions carefully.
- If a question contains a choice, be sure to spend a minute or two making the best choice for you.
- In experimental questions, you must be aware of what variables are, why controls are needed and how reliability and validity might be improved. It is worth spending time on these ideas – they are essential and will come up year after year.
- Some candidates like to use a highlighter pen to help them focus on the essential points of longer questions – this is a great technique.
- Remember that a conclusion can be seen from data, whereas an explanation will usually require you to supply some background knowledge as well.
- If you are asked to draw a conclusion, make sure you relate it to any aim stated in the question.
- Remember to use values and units from the graph when describing graphical information in words if you are asked to do so.
- Plot graphs carefully and join the plot points using a ruler. Include zeros on your scale where appropriate and use the data table headings for the axes labels.
- Look out for graphs with two Y-axes – these need extra special concentration and anyone can make a mistake!
- If there is a space for calculation given – you will very likely need to use it! A calculator is essential.
- The main types of calculation tend to be ratios, averages, percentages and percentage change – make sure you can do these common calculations.
- Answers to calculations will not usually have more than two decimal places.
- Do not leave blanks. Always have a go, using the language in the question if you can.

Good luck!

Remember that the rewards for passing Higher Biology are well worth it! Your pass will help you get the future you want for yourself. In the exam, be confident in your own ability. If you're not sure how to answer a question, trust your instincts and just give it a go anyway.

Keep calm and don't panic! GOOD LUCK!

Study Skills – what you need to know to pass exams!

General exam revision: 20 top tips

When preparing for exams, it is easy to feel unsure of where to start or how to revise. This guide to general exam revision provides a good starting place, and, as these are very general tips, they can be applied to all your exams.

1. Start revising in good time.

Don't leave revision until the last minute – this will make you panic and it will be difficult to learn. Make a revision timetable that counts down the weeks to go.

2. Work to a study plan.

Set up sessions of work spread through the weeks ahead. Make sure each session has a focus and a clear purpose. What will you study, when and why? Be realistic about what you can achieve in each session, and don't be afraid to adjust your plans as needed.

3. Make sure you know exactly when your exams are.

Get your exam dates from the SQA website and use the timetable builder tool to create your own exam schedule. You will also get a personalised timetable from your school, but this might not be until close to the exam period.

4. Make sure that you know the topics that make up each course.

Studying is easier if material is in manageable chunks – why not use the SQA topic headings or create your own from your class notes? Ask your teacher for help on this if you are not sure.

5. Break the chunks up into even smaller bits.

The small chunks should be easier to cope with. Remember that they fit together to make larger ideas. Even the process of chunking down will help!

6. Ask yourself these key questions for each course:

- Are all topics compulsory or are there choices?
- Which topics seem to come up time and time again?
- Which topics are your strongest and which are your weakest?

Use your answers to these questions to work out how much time you will need to spend revising each topic.

7. Make sure you know what to expect in the exam.

The subject-specific introduction to this book will help with this. Make sure you can answer these questions:

- How is the paper structured?
- How much time is there for each part of the exam?
- What types of question are involved? These will vary depending on the subject so read the subject-specific section carefully.

8. Past papers are a vital revision tool!

Use past papers to support your revision wherever possible. This book contains the answers and mark schemes too – refer to these carefully when checking your work. Using the mark scheme is useful; even if you don't manage to get all the marks available first time when you first practise, it helps you identify how to extend and develop your answers to get more marks next time – and of course, in the real exam.

9. Use study methods that work well for you.

People study and learn in different ways. Reading and looking at diagrams suits some students. Others prefer to listen and hear material – what about reading out loud or getting a friend or family member to do this for you? You could also record and play back material.

10. There are three tried and tested ways to make material stick in your long-term memory:

- Practising – e.g. rehearsal, repeating
- Organising – e.g. making drawings, lists, diagrams, tables, memory aids
- Elaborating – e.g. incorporating the material into a story or an imagined journey

11. Learn actively.

Most people prefer to learn actively – for example, making notes, highlighting, redrawing and redrafting, making up memory aids, or writing past paper answers. A good way to stay engaged and inspired is to mix and match these methods – find the combination that best suits you. This is likely to vary depending on the topic or subject.

12. Be an expert.

Be sure to have a few areas in which you feel you are an expert. This often works because at least some of them will come up, which can boost confidence.

13. Try some visual methods.

Use symbols, diagrams, charts, flashcards, post-it notes etc. Don't forget – the brain takes in chunked images more easily than loads of text.

14. Remember – practice makes perfect.

Work on difficult areas again and again. Look and read – then test yourself. You cannot do this too much.

15. Try past papers against the clock.

Practise writing answers in a set time. This is a good habit from the start but is especially important when you get closer to exam time.

16. Collaborate with friends.

Test each other and talk about the material – this can really help. Two brains are better than one! It is amazing how talking about a problem can help you solve it.

17. Know your weaknesses.

Ask your teacher for help to identify what you don't know. Try to do this as early as possible. If you are having trouble, it is probably with a difficult topic, so your teacher will already be aware of this – most students will find it tough.

18. Have your materials organised and ready.

Know what is needed for each exam:

- Do you need a calculator or a ruler?
- Should you have pencils as well as pens?
- Will you need water or paper tissues?

19. Make full use of school resources.

Find out what support is on offer:

- Are there study classes available?
- When is the library open?
- When is the best time to ask for extra help?
- Can you borrow textbooks, study guides, past papers, etc.?
- Is school open for Easter revision?

20. Keep fit and healthy!

Try to stick to a routine as much as possible, including with sleep. If you are tired, sluggish or dehydrated, it is difficult to see how concentration is even possible. Combine study with relaxation, drink plenty of water, eat sensibly, and get fresh air and exercise – all these things will help more than you could imagine. Good luck!

HIGHER

2017

National Qualifications 2017

X707/76/02

Biology
Section 1 — Questions

TUESDAY, 23 MAY

9:00 AM — 11:30 AM

Instructions for the completion of Section 1 are given on *Page two* of your question and answer booklet X707/76/01.

Record your answers on the answer grid on *Page three* of your question and answer booklet.

Before leaving the examination room you must give your question and answer booklet to the Invigilator; if you do not, you may lose all the marks for this paper.

SECTION 1 — 20 marks

Attempt ALL questions

1. Which of the following diagrams shows the correct structure of DNA?

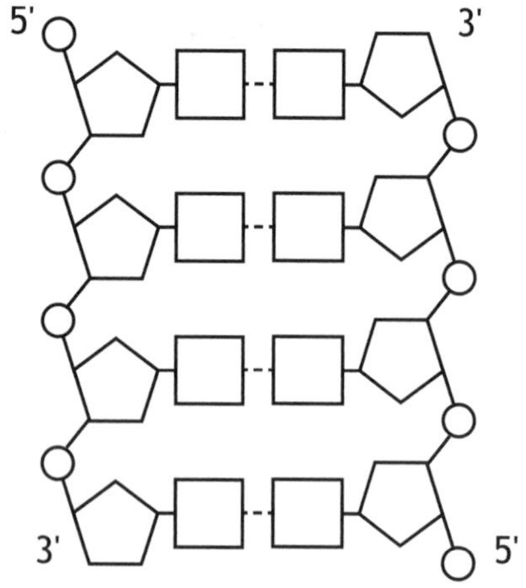

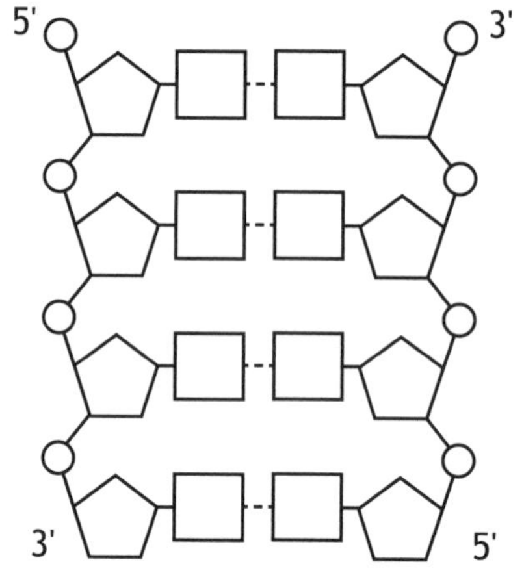

2. A section of double stranded DNA was found to have 60 guanine bases and 30 adenine bases.

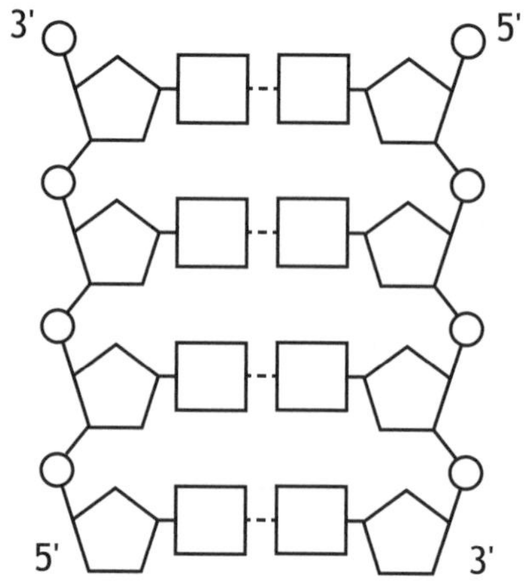

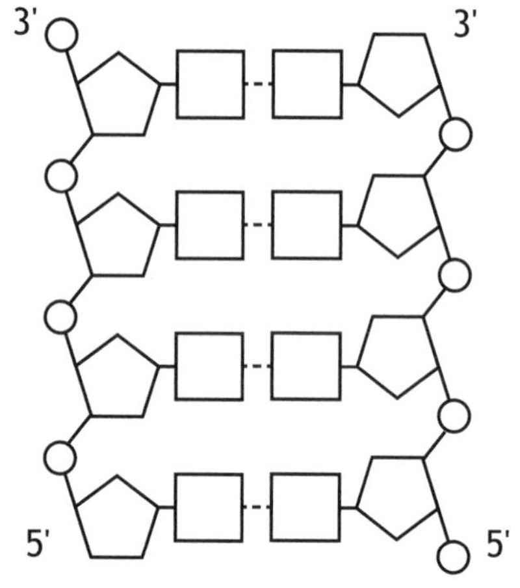

   What is the total number of deoxyribose sugars in this section?

   A   30

   B   90

   C   180

   D   270

3. The following terms describe different structures into which DNA can be organised within cells.

    1   Linear chromosome

    2   Circular chromosome

    3   Circular plasmid

    Which of these terms describe how DNA is organised within photosynthetic plant cells?

    A   1 only

    B   2 only

    C   1 and 2 only

    D   2 and 3 only

4. Which of the following molecules are required in the replication of the lagging strand of a DNA molecule?

    A   DNA polymerase and ligase only

    B   DNA polymerase and primers only

    C   Ligase and primers only

    D   DNA polymerase, ligase and primers

[Turn over

5. The diagram shows a molecule of tRNA.

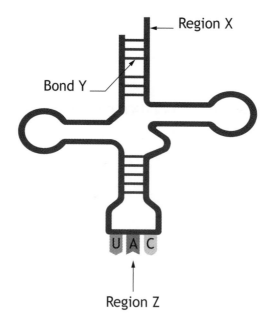

Which row in the table identifies Region X, Bond Y and Region Z?

	Region X	Bond Y	Region Z
A	amino acid attachment site	hydrogen	anticodon
B	anticodon	hydrogen	amino acid attachment site
C	amino acid attachment site	peptide	anticodon
D	anticodon	peptide	amino acid attachment site

6. New species have evolved when two populations have become

A   isolated by a behavioural barrier

B   unable to interbreed to produce fertile offspring

C   very different due to directional selection

D   very different due to disruptive selection.

7. The diagram shows an enzyme, its substrate and a substance which inhibits it.

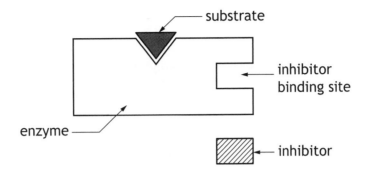

The following statements describe some features of enzyme inhibition.

1   The inhibitor binds to the active site.

2   The effect of the inhibitor is reduced by increasing the substrate concentration.

3   The inhibitor is non-competitive.

Which of these statements apply to the inhibitor shown in the diagram?

A   1 only

B   3 only

C   1 and 2 only

D   2 and 3 only

[Turn over

8. An investigation was carried out to determine the effect of lead ion concentration on the activity of the enzyme amylase.

   The results are shown in the table.

Lead ion concentration (mol l^{-1})	Amylase activity (% of control)
0·0 (control)	100
0·1	84
0·2	23
0·3	11
0·4	2
0·5	0

   A conclusion that can be drawn from these results is that inhibition was

   A highest at high lead ion concentrations

   B highest at low lead ion concentrations

   C lowest at lead ion concentration 0·5 mol l^{-1}

   D highest at lead ion concentration 0·1 mol l^{-1}.

9. ATP is recycled to transfer energy within cells. The diagram shows two reactions involving ATP.

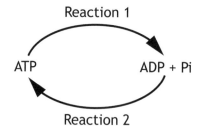

Reaction 1

ATP   ADP + Pi

Reaction 2

   Which row in the table describes Reaction 1 and Reaction 2?

	Reaction 1	Reaction 2
A	catabolic and energy released	anabolic and energy required
B	anabolic and energy released	catabolic and energy required
C	catabolic and energy required	anabolic and energy released
D	anabolic and energy required	catabolic and energy released

10. The fungus *Aspergillus niger* is grown in large fermenters to produce citric acid using starch as a substrate.

The graph shows the changes in the citric acid and starch concentrations in a fermenter over 168 hours.

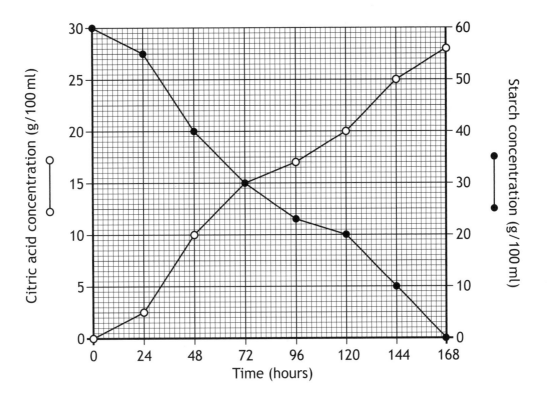

The citric acid concentration equals the starch concentration at

A   0 hours

B   48 hours

C   72 hours

D   120 hours.

[Turn over

11. The following list describes changes which take place during temperature regulation in mammals.

    1   Vasodilation

    2   Vasoconstriction

    3   Contraction of hair erector muscles

    4   Relaxation of hair erector muscles

    Which of these changes takes place in response to a decrease in body temperature?

    A   1 and 3 only

    B   1 and 4 only

    C   2 and 3 only

    D   2 and 4 only

12. The diagram shows a bacterial plasmid with restriction sites for three different restriction endonucleases, Sal1, Eco R1 and Bam H1.

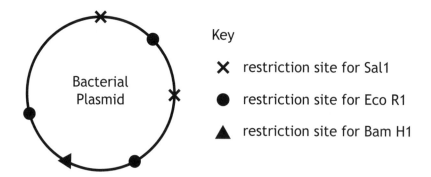

Key

✗ restriction site for Sal1

● restriction site for Eco R1

▲ restriction site for Bam H1

    Which row in the table identifies the number of fragments produced if the plasmid was cut with the combinations of restriction endonucleases shown?

	Combination	
	Sal1 and Bam H1	Sal1 and Eco R1
A	3	4
B	3	5
C	4	4
D	4	5

13. Inbreeding depression is a result of

   A   an increase in heterozygotes

   B   a genetically variable population

   C   crossbreeding for improved characteristics

   D   an accumulation of recessive deleterious alleles.

14. Livestock production generates less food per unit area of land than crop production because

   A   energy is gained between trophic levels of the food chain

   B   livestock production degrades natural resources

   C   energy is lost between trophic levels of the food chain

   D   it is easier to grow crops than raise livestock in difficult habitats.

15. The table shows optimum, maximum and minimum temperatures for the growth of some crop plants.

Crop	Temperature (°C)		
	Optimum	Maximum	Minimum
Maize	22–26	32–34	20–22
Wheat	20–25	36–38	5–7
Rice	30–33	37–40	18–22
Potato	15–20	28–34	12–14
Soyabean	25–28	37–40	10–14

Which of the following predictions is supported by the evidence in the table?

   A   Maize will grow at lower temperatures than soyabean.

   B   Rice will grow at higher temperatures than soyabean.

   C   Rice will grow in a narrower range of temperatures than maize.

   D   Wheat will grow in a wider range of temperatures than potato.

[Turn over

16. Triticale is a hybrid cereal species which was produced by crossing *Triticum durum* (a species of wheat) with *Secale cereale* (a species of rye) as shown in the diagram.

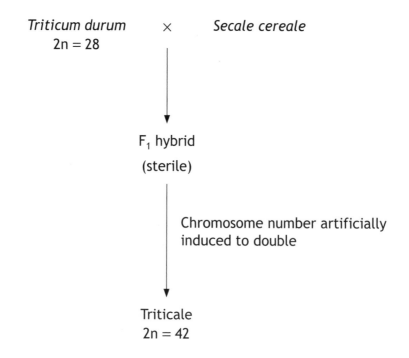

Triticum durum × *Secale cereale*
2n = 28

F₁ hybrid
(sterile)

Chromosome number artificially induced to double

Triticale
2n = 42

What was the diploid (2n) number of chromosomes in *Secale cereale*?

A 7

B 14

C 21

D 28

17. The following statements describe symbiotic relationships between organisms.

1 Mistletoe plants absorb nutrients from apple trees on which they grow.

2 Egyptian Plover birds clean the teeth of Nile crocodiles and feed on the debris they remove.

3 Tapeworms live in the small intestine of pigs and absorb some of their nutrients.

Which of these relationships can be described as parasitic?

A 2 only

B 3 only

C 1 and 2 only

D 1 and 3 only

18. Resveratrol is a substance which may reduce the risk of heart disease. Using recombinant DNA technology, *E. coli* bacteria have been modified so that they now produce resveratrol when grown in a medium containing coumaric acid.

    The graph shows concentrations of resveratrol and coumaric acid in the medium over a 30 hour period.

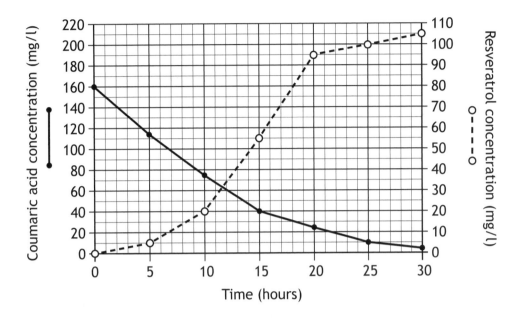

    The simplest whole number ratio of the concentration of resveratrol to coumaric acid after 25 hours is

    A   1 : 2

    B   1 : 40

    C   10 : 1

    D   20 : 1.

19. Which row in the table identifies how the bottleneck effect and habitat corridors may change genetic diversity of a population?

	Change in genetic diversity	
	Bottleneck effect	Habitat corridors
A	decrease	decrease
B	decrease	increase
C	increase	decrease
D	increase	increase

[Turn over

20. Some species of social insect are of economic importance to humans by providing ecosystem services.

Which of the following are examples of ecosystem services?

1   Braconid wasps parasitising hornworms which are a pest of tomatoes.

2   Bumblebees pollinating an orchard of apple trees.

3   Worker termites caring for the queen and her offspring.

A   1 and 2 only

B   1 and 3 only

C   2 and 3 only

D   1, 2 and 3

[END OF SECTION 1. NOW ATTEMPT THE QUESTIONS IN SECTION 2 OF YOUR QUESTION AND ANSWER BOOKLET.]

National
Qualifications
2017

Mark

X707/76/01

Biology
Section 1 — Answer Grid
and Section 2

TUESDAY, 23 MAY

9:00 AM – 11:30 AM

Fill in these boxes and read what is printed below.

Full name of centre

Town

Forename(s)

Surname

Number of seat

Date of birth

Day	Month	Year

Scottish candidate number

Total marks — 100

SECTION 1 — 20 marks

Attempt ALL questions.

Instructions for the completion of Section 1 are given on *Page two*.

SECTION 2 — 80 marks

Attempt ALL questions.

Questions 10 and 15 contain a choice.

Write your answers clearly in the spaces provided in this booklet. Additional space for answers and rough work is provided at the end of this booklet. If you use this space you must clearly identify the question number you are attempting. Any rough work must be written in this booklet. You should score through your rough work when you have written your final copy.

Use **blue** or **black** ink.

Before leaving the examination room you must give this booklet to the Invigilator; if you do not, you may lose all the marks for this paper.

SECTION 1 — 20 marks

The questions for Section 1 are contained in the question paper X707/76/02.

Read these and record your answers on the answer grid on *Page three* opposite.

Use **blue** or **black** ink. Do NOT use gel pens or pencil.

1. The answer to each question is **either** A, B, C or D. Decide what your answer is, then fill in the appropriate bubble (see sample question below).

2. There is **only one correct** answer to each question.

3. Any rough working should be done on the additional space for answers and rough work at the end of this booklet.

Sample Question

The thigh bone is called the

    A   humerus

    B   femur

    C   tibia

    D   fibula.

The correct answer is **B** — femur. The answer **B** bubble has been clearly filled in (see below).

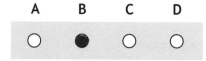

Changing an answer

If you decide to change your answer, cancel your first answer by putting a cross through it (see below) and fill in the answer you want. The answer below has been changed to **D**.

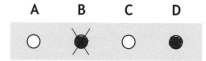

If you then decide to change back to an answer you have already scored out, put a tick (✓) to the **right** of the answer you want, as shown below:

SECTION 1 — Answer Grid

	A	B	C	D
1	○	○	○	○
2	○	○	○	○
3	○	○	○	○
4	○	○	○	○
5	○	○	○	○
6	○	○	○	○
7	○	○	○	○
8	○	○	○	○
9	○	○	○	○
10	○	○	○	○
11	○	○	○	○
12	○	○	○	○
13	○	○	○	○
14	○	○	○	○
15	○	○	○	○
16	○	○	○	○
17	○	○	○	○
18	○	○	○	○
19	○	○	○	○
20	○	○	○	○

[BLANK PAGE]

DO NOT WRITE ON THIS PAGE

[Turn over for next question

DO NOT WRITE ON THIS PAGE

MARKS | DO NOT WRITE IN THIS MARGIN

SECTION 2 — 80 marks

Attempt ALL questions

Note that Questions 10 and 15 contain a choice

1. The diagram illustrates steps in the transcription and translation of a gene.

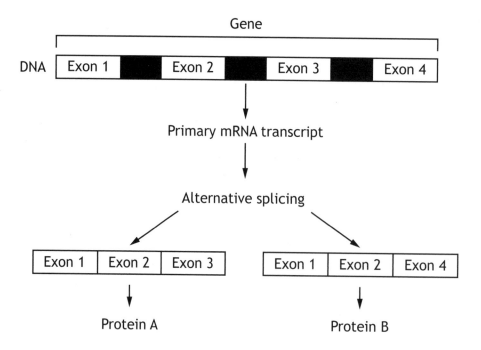

Gene

DNA | Exon 1 | | Exon 2 | | Exon 3 | | Exon 4 |

Primary mRNA transcript

Alternative splicing

| Exon 1 | Exon 2 | Exon 3 | | Exon 1 | Exon 2 | Exon 4 |

Protein A   Protein B

(a) Name the regions always removed from a primary mRNA transcript.   **1**

_____

(b) Insert numbers in the boxes below to show the three exons in the gene shown above which could be translated to produce a protein which is different from proteins A and B.   **1**

| Exon _____ | Exon _____ | Exon _____ |

1. **(continued)**

   (c) Single gene mutations can occur which may affect the structure of the proteins produced.

   (i) Describe the effect of a nonsense mutation on Protein A and give a reason for your answer.

   2

   Description _____

   _____

   Reason _____

   _____

   (ii) A deletion mutation occurred in Exon 2.

   Explain why this would have a major effect on the structure of proteins A and B.

   1

   _____

   _____

   _____

   [Turn over

MARKS | DO NOT WRITE IN THIS MARGIN

2. Two heat-tolerant DNA polymerases used in polymerase chain reactions (PCR) are *Taq* and *Pfu*.

    Pfu has "proof reading" activity. It checks that the correct nucleotides are inserted during replication of a target sequence and then corrects any errors.

    The graph shows the temperatures during a single PCR cycle required to amplify a target sequence using *Taq* and *Pfu*.

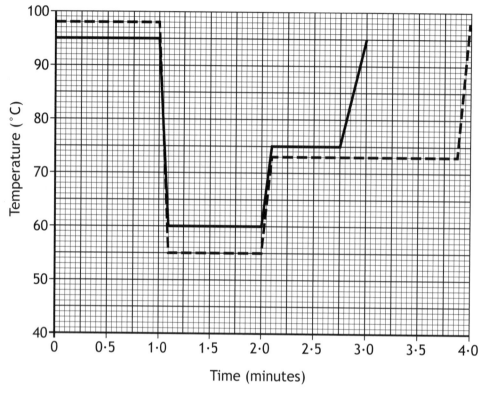

    Key: ———— *Taq* polymerase

          - - - - *Pfu* polymerase

    (a) (i) Calculate the time taken for 16 copies of the target sequence to be made from one DNA fragment using *Taq* polymerase.   1

             Space for calculation

             _____ minutes

MARKS | DO NOT WRITE IN THIS MARGIN

2. (a) (continued)

(ii) Identify the time period during which primers bind to the original DNA fragment.   **1**

from _____ to _____ minutes.

(b) A scientist was planning to amplify DNA using PCR.

State which DNA polymerase should be used and describe the advantage of using this polymerase.   **1**

DNA polymerase _____

Advantage _____

_____

(c) Explain the importance of using heat-tolerant DNA polymerases in PCR.   **1**

_____

_____

[Turn over

MARKS | DO NOT WRITE IN THIS MARGIN

3. The herbicide glyphosate is used to control the annual weed charlock (*Sinapis arvensis*) in cereal fields.

An investigation was carried out into the effect of glyphosate on the development of glyphosate resistance in charlock plants in a cereal plot.

The charlock plants were treated with glyphosate from 2009 to 2016 and the percentage of glyphosate resistant plants in the plot was recorded every year.

The results are shown in the table.

Year	Charlock plants resistant to glyphosate (%)
2009	10
2010	18
2011	32
2012	42
2013	53
2014	58
2015	66
2016	66

(a) Using values from the table describe the change in glyphosate resistance over the time of investigation.   2

_____

_____

_____

_____

(b) Explain how natural selection resulted in the change in glyphosate resistance.   2

_____

_____

_____

_____

(c) Another investigation was carried out into the development of antibiotic resistance in bacteria. It was observed to be more rapid than the development of glyphosate resistance in charlock.

Explain this observation in terms of gene transfer.   1

_____

_____

MARKS | DO NOT WRITE IN THIS MARGIN

4. (a) Human muscles contain satellite cells within the muscle tissue.

The diagram illustrates the division and differentiation of satellite cells.

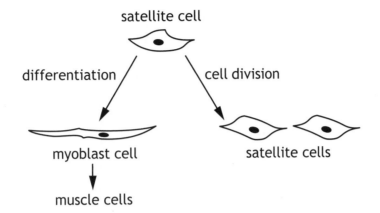

(i) Using information from the diagram explain why satellite cells are an example of tissue (adult) and not embryonic stem cells.

1

_____

_____

(ii) State **one** benefit to the human body of satellite cells differentiating into myoblast cells.

1

_____

_____

(iii) Satellite cells could be used to treat muscle diseases.

Give **one** ethical reason for using satellite cells instead of embryonic stem cells in order to treat such diseases.

1

_____

_____

(b) Give **one** example of how stem cells are used as model cells in medical research.

1

_____

_____

[Turn over

MARKS | DO NOT WRITE IN THIS MARGIN

5. (a) The phylogenetic tree illustrates the evolutionary relatedness of six groups of animals.

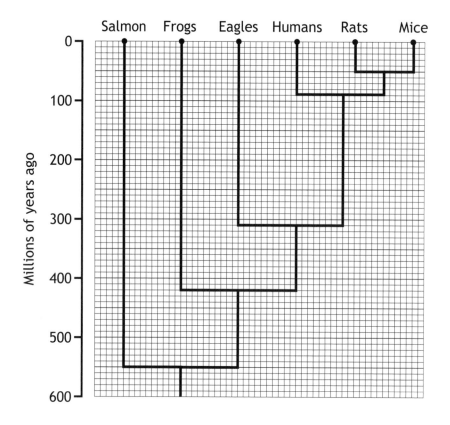

(i) Using information from the phylogenetic tree state when the last common ancestor of salmon and frogs lived.   1

_____million years ago

(ii) Calculate how many million years separate the divergence of eagles and humans from the divergence of rats and mice.   1

Space for calculation

_____ million years

(iii) Rats are more closely related to humans than they are to frogs.

Use evidence from the phylogenetic tree to justify this statement.   1

_____

_____

MARKS | DO NOT WRITE IN THIS MARGIN

5. (continued)

(b) The graph shows a molecular clock which compares the amino acid sequence of the protein cytochrome c between a range of species.

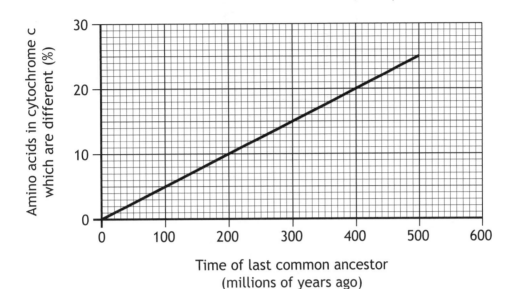

(i) Cytochrome c is a protein containing 112 amino acids.

Calculate the number of amino acids in cytochrome c that are different between two species whose last common ancestor lived 500 million years ago.

Space for calculation

1

_____

(ii) Predict the percentage of amino acids in cytochrome c which would be different between two species who shared a common ancestor 550 million years ago.

1

_____ %

(c) Using information from the **phylogenetic tree and the graph**, state the percentage of amino acids in cytochrome c that are different between rats and frogs.

1

_____ %

MARKS | DO NOT WRITE IN THIS MARGIN

6. The diagram shows genetically modified yeast growing in a fermenter in a medium to which the amino acid lysine has been added.

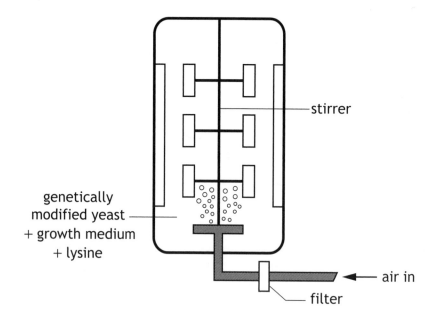

genetically modified yeast + growth medium + lysine

—stirrer

← air in

filter

(a) (i) Name the process for which the yeast cells need the amino acid lysine.   1

_____

(ii) The fermenter contains 5·5 litres of growth medium.

Calculate the mass of lysine which should be added to the medium to give a concentration of 300 mg/l.   1

Space for calculation

_____ mg

(iii) The air entering the fermenter passes through a filter to prevent contamination.

Explain why it is necessary to prevent contamination of the culture.   1

_____

_____

MARKS | DO NOT WRITE IN THIS MARGIN

6. (a) (continued)

(iv) The optimum pH for yeast growth is 4·5.

Suggest how this pH could be maintained in the fermenter.   1

_____

(b) Some phases of a growth curve of yeast culture are shown.

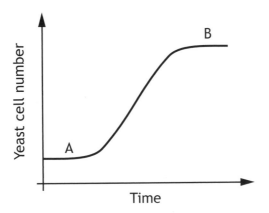

Complete the table by selecting growth phase A **or** B. Name the chosen phase and describe an event which occurs during that phase of growth.   2

Letter	Phase of growth	Description

(c) Describe a safety mechanism used to prevent the survival of genetically modified microorganisms in the external environment.   1

_____

_____

[Turn over

MARKS | DO NOT WRITE IN THIS MARGIN

7. Sea bass are saltwater fish that can regulate their internal salt concentration. They have specialised cells in their gills with protein pumps in the membrane. These pumps actively transport excess salt from their bodies.

(a) The specialised cells have many mitochondria.

Explain why this is necessary. **2**

_____

_____

_____

(b) Many animal species regulate their body temperature.

Explain the importance of regulating body temperature. **1**

_____

_____

_____

(c) Compare regulators and conformers in terms of their ecological niches. **1**

_____

_____

_____

[Turn over for next question

DO NOT WRITE ON THIS PAGE

MARKS | DO NOT WRITE IN THIS MARGIN

8. Deer mice (*Peromyscus maniculatus*) are small mammals living in a variety of habitats ranging from low to high altitude.

An investigation was carried out to compare the haemoglobin from two populations of deer mice living at low and high altitudes.

Blood samples were taken from both populations and exposed to different levels of oxygen. The percentage of haemoglobin in the blood samples which had oxygen bound to it was measured.

The results are shown in the graph.

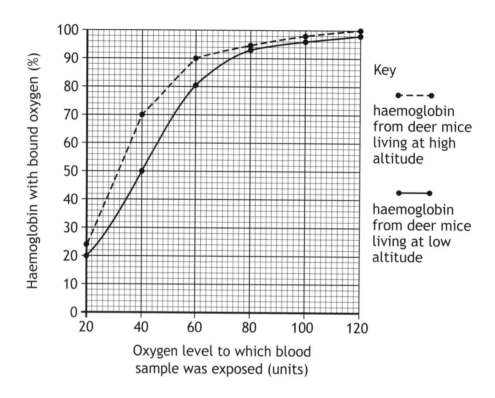

Key

- - -
haemoglobin from deer mice living at high altitude

——
haemoglobin from deer mice living at low altitude

(a) (i) State **one** variable that should be controlled when exposing the blood samples to oxygen in order for a valid conclusion to be drawn.

1

_____

MARKS | DO NOT WRITE IN THIS MARGIN

8. (a) (continued)

(ii) State the oxygen level at which there is the greatest difference in the percentage of haemoglobin bound to oxygen between the two groups.   **1**

_____ units

(iii) Use information from the graph to explain how the deer mice from the population living at high altitude are adapted to a low oxygen niche.   **1**

_____

_____

(b) Suggest **one** physiological adaptation, other than differences in haemoglobin, that deer mice from high altitudes could have to increase the efficiency of oxygen delivery to cells.   **1**

_____

_____

(c) Describe the structure of a deer mouse heart and explain how this allows efficient delivery of oxygen to cells.   **2**

Description _____

_____

Explanation _____

_____

[Turn over

MARKS | DO NOT WRITE IN THIS MARGIN

9. Catalase is an enzyme which breaks down hydrogen peroxide into oxygen and water. Paper discs soaked in catalase sink when placed into hydrogen peroxide solution. The discs rise to the surface when oxygen is produced. The time taken for the discs to rise can be used to measure catalase activity.

An experiment was set up to investigate the effect of copper sulfate concentration on catalase activity.

Six tubes were set up, each containing $10\,cm^3$ of hydrogen peroxide and $5\,cm^3$ of a different concentration of copper sulfate. One paper disc was then placed into each test tube as shown in the diagram. The time taken for each paper disc to rise to the surface was recorded.

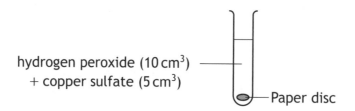

hydrogen peroxide ($10\,cm^3$)
+ copper sulfate ($5\,cm^3$) ————— Paper disc

The results are shown in the table.

Concentration of copper sulfate solution $(mol\,l^{-1})$	Time taken for paper disc to rise (seconds)
0·2	8
0·3	12
0·4	15
0·6	18
0·8	19
1·0	20

(a) (i) Name the independent variable in this experiment. 　1

_____

(ii) Describe a suitable control for this experiment. 　1

_____

_____

(iii) Suggest how the temperature of the tubes could be kept constant. 　1

_____

_____

MARKS | DO NOT WRITE IN THIS MARGIN

9. (a) (continued)

(iv) Give a feature of the experiment which may make the results unreliable.

1

_____

_____

(b) (i) Draw a line graph using the results in the table.

(Additional graph paper, if required, will be found on *Page thirty-two.*)

2

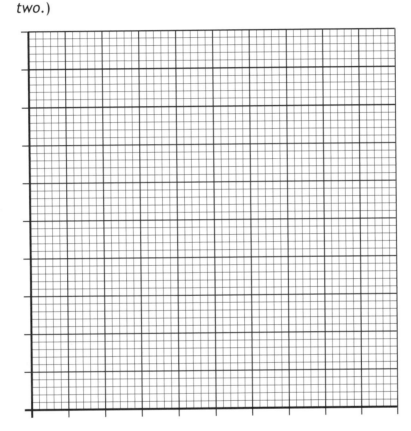

(ii) Calculate the percentage increase in the time taken for the paper disc to rise when the copper sulfate concentration increased from $0.2\,mol\,l^{-1}$ to $1.0\,mol\,l^{-1}$.

1

Space for calculation

_____ %

(c) Draw a conclusion from the results of this experiment.

1

_____

_____

[Turn over

MARKS | DO NOT WRITE IN THIS MARGIN

10. Answer **either A or B** in the space below.

A   Write notes on primate behaviour.   4

OR

B   Write notes on invasive species.   4

MARKS | DO NOT WRITE IN THIS MARGIN

11. During photosynthesis light energy is absorbed by photosynthetic pigments in the chloroplasts.

(a) (i) State one fate of the light which is **not** absorbed by the photosynthetic pigments.

1

_____

(ii) Describe the effect of absorbed light energy on the pigment molecules.

1

_____

_____

(iii) Plants contain several pigments including chlorophyll a, chlorophyll b and carotenoids. Explain the advantage to a plant of having more than one type of photosynthetic pigment.

1

_____

_____

(b) Following photolysis, hydrogen is transferred to the coenzyme NADP.

State the source of this hydrogen.

1

_____

(c) Describe the role of the NADPH in the Calvin cycle (carbon fixation).

1

_____

_____

[Turn over

MARKS | DO NOT WRITE IN THIS MARGIN

12. Potato plants are attacked by leaf eating caterpillars. *Bacillus thuringiensis* is a bacterium which can be used to control these pests. The bacteria produce a protein (Bt toxin) which kills these caterpillars.

(a) (i) Explain how an attack by leaf eating caterpillars causes a reduction in crop yield.

2

_____

_____

_____

(ii) State an advantage of using this type of biological control rather than using chemicals.

1

_____

_____

(b) Bt toxin does not kill all caterpillars.

A study was carried out to investigate the effectiveness of the Bt toxin compared with a modified Bt toxin by exposing different groups of caterpillars to them.

The results are shown in the table.

Toxin tested	Number of caterpillars tested	Number of caterpillars surviving	Caterpillars killed (%)
Bt toxin alone	240	204	
Modified Bt toxin alone	300	105	65
Bt toxin and modified Bt toxin used together	210	42	80

(i) Complete the table to show the percentage of caterpillars killed by the Bt toxin alone.

1

Space for calculation

MARKS | DO NOT WRITE IN THIS MARGIN

12.   (b)   (continued)

(ii)   The Bt toxin and modified Bt toxin work by different mechanisms.
Use information from the table to justify this statement.

1

_____

_____

_____

[Turn over

MARKS | DO NOT WRITE IN THIS MARGIN

13. Gluten is a protein found in crops that can cause human health problems. Scientists are breeding barley cultivars to produce ultra low gluten levels.

A commercially produced barley (Sloop) and a low gluten cultivar (LG) were crossed to produce two different cultivars with ultra low gluten levels (ULG 1 and ULG 2).

The gluten content of each cultivar is shown in the table.

Barley cultivar	Gluten content (mg/g)
Sloop	57·0
LG	5·1
ULG 1	1·7
ULG 2	0·004

(a) Calculate how many times greater the gluten content of Sloop is compared to that of ULG 2.   **1**

Space for calculation

_____ times greater

(b) The allele for ultra low gluten is recessive. To investigate if the cultivar LG was heterozygous for gluten, it was crossed with the cultivar ULG1 which was homozygous for this recessive allele.

low gluten   ×   ULG1
cultivar
↓
offspring

(i) Name this type of cross.   **1**

_____

(ii) Describe the expected phenotypes of the offspring if LG was heterozygous.   **1**

_____

_____

MARKS | DO NOT WRITE IN THIS MARGIN

13.   (continued)

(c)   Barley is a naturally inbreeding plant.

Explain why inbreeding depression would be unlikely to be a problem when a barley cultivar self-pollinates for many generations.   **1**

_____

_____

(d)   Barley grains contain the enzyme amylase which breaks down starch in the grain to sugar used in brewing beer.

Average grain mass, starch content and amylase activity for three barley cultivars are shown in the table.

Barley cultivar	Average mass of a single grain (mg)	Starch content of grains (%)	Amylase activity (units/mg)
Sloop	53·6	70	0·6
ULG1	33·5	65	1·0
ULG2	39·2	64	1·4

(i)   As well as total mass of all the grains, state the information required in order to calculate the average mass of a single grain.   **1**

_____

(ii)   Select a cultivar from the table that would be best to use in beer production and justify your selection.   **1**

Cultivar _____

Justification _____

_____

[Turn over

MARKS | DO NOT WRITE IN THIS MARGIN

14. African wild dogs are carnivores which live in packs and use cooperative hunting. Each wild dog requires an average of 30 000 kJ of energy per day for the pack to survive.

The bar chart shows the relationship between pack size and energy gain per wild dog per day.

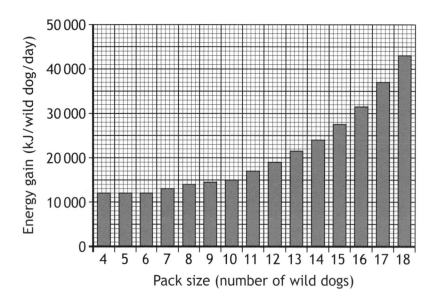

(a) Using information from the bar chart, state the minimum pack size

   (i) at which cooperative hunting becomes an advantage;   1

   _____ wild dogs

   (ii) for survival of the pack.   1

   _____ wild dogs

(b) Suggest why wild dogs in larger packs gain more energy per individual from hunting even though there are more animals to be fed.   1

_____

_____

(c) Most of the wild dogs in a pack are related. Usually only one dominant female has offspring which other members of the pack will feed.

Explain why pack members feed offspring which are not their own.   1

_____

_____

MARKS | DO NOT WRITE IN THIS MARGIN

15. Answer **either A or B** in the space below and on *Pages thirty* and *thirty-one*.

A   Write notes on the citric acid cycle of cell respiration.   **7**

OR

B   Write notes on how animals survive and avoid adverse conditions.   **7**

MARKS | DO NOT WRITE IN THIS MARGIN

SPACE FOR ANSWERS

MARKS | DO NOT WRITE IN THIS MARGIN

SPACE FOR ANSWERS

[END OF QUESTION PAPER]

MARKS | DO NOT WRITE IN THIS MARGIN

ADDITIONAL SPACE FOR ANSWERS AND ROUGH WORK

ADDITIONAL GRAPH PAPER FOR QUESTION 9 (b) (i)

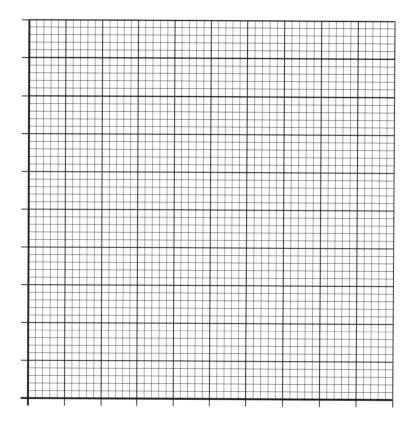

HIGHER

2018

National
Qualifications
2018

X707/76/02

Biology
Section 1 — Questions

TUESDAY, 15 MAY

9:00 AM – 11:30 AM

Instructions for the completion of Section 1 are given on *Page two* of your question and answer booklet X707/76/01.

Record your answers on the answer grid on *Page three* of your question and answer booklet.

Before leaving the examination room you must give your question and answer booklet to the Invigilator; if you do not, you may lose all the marks for this paper.

SECTION 1 — 20 marks
Attempt ALL questions

1. The following substances are products of fermentation.

   1   ATP

   2   Lactate

   3   Carbon dioxide

   Which of these are products of fermentation in human muscle cells?

   A   2 only

   B   1 and 2 only

   C   2 and 3 only

   D   1, 2 and 3

2. The diagram represents a stage of cellular respiration that occurs in a mitochondrion.

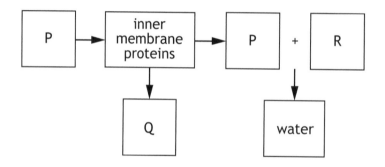

   Which row in the table identifies substances P, Q and R?

	Substances		
	P	Q	R
A	ATP	hydrogen ions and electrons	oxygen
B	hydrogen ions and electrons	oxygen	ATP
C	oxygen	ATP	hydrogen ions and electrons
D	hydrogen ions and electrons	ATP	oxygen

3. Part of a metabolic pathway used by cells to produce the amino acid alanine is shown.

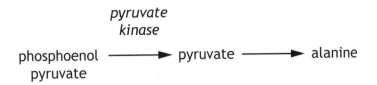

Alanine is a non-competitive, feedback inhibitor of the enzyme pyruvate kinase.

The following statements refer to the metabolic pathway.

1   Pyruvate kinase reduces the activation energy needed to convert phosphoenol pyruvate into pyruvate.

2   Phosphoenol pyruvate is the substrate for pyruvate kinase.

3   Alanine can bind to the active site of pyruvate kinase.

Which of these statements are correct?

A   1 and 2 only

B   1 and 3 only

C   2 and 3 only

D   1, 2 and 3

[Turn over

4. Shrews are small mammals. The graph shows the relationship between body mass and oxygen consumption of shrews at two environmental temperatures.

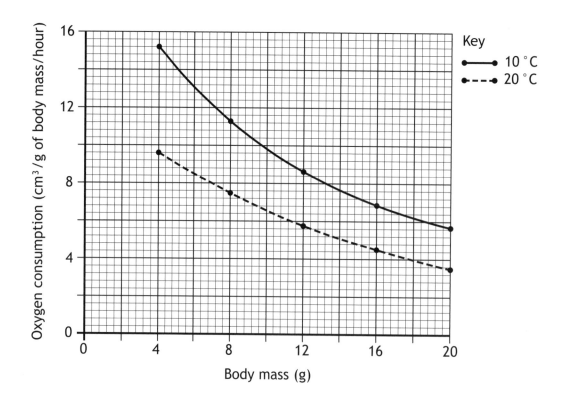

Which of the following statements about this graph is correct?

A   Shrews of greater mass consumed less oxygen.

B   The optimum temperature for oxygen consumption was 10 °C.

C   As environmental temperature increased oxygen consumption decreased.

D   At 10 °C a 16 g shrew consumed $6.2 \, cm^3$ of oxygen/g of body mass/hour.

5. Yeast cells contain the enzyme catalase which breaks down hydrogen peroxide to produce oxygen. An experiment was carried out into the effect of lead nitrate concentration on the activity of catalase.

Six flasks were set up. Each contained $25 \, cm^3$ of hydrogen peroxide and $10 \, cm^3$ of yeast suspension. $10 \, cm^3$ of a different concentration of lead nitrate was then added to each flask. The volume of oxygen produced after 15 minutes was measured.

Identify the independent variable in this experiment.

A   Volume of lead nitrate

B   Volume of oxygen produced

C   Activity of catalase

D   Concentration of lead nitrate

6. The diagram illustrates the circulatory system of a fish. The arrows indicate the direction of blood flow.

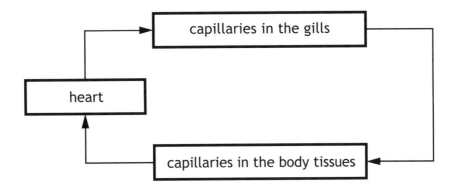

Which row in the table describes the type of circulatory system of a fish and the blood pressure in the capillaries in the gills and body tissues?

	Type of circulatory system	Blood pressure in the capillaries in the gills	Blood pressure in the capillaries in the body tissues
A	single	lower	higher
B	double	higher	lower
C	single	higher	lower
D	double	lower	higher

[Turn over

7. In an investigation into fermentation, yeast was grown in a flask of glucose solution for 20 hours at 20°C.

The graph shows the concentrations of ethanol and glucose in the flask over the period of the investigation.

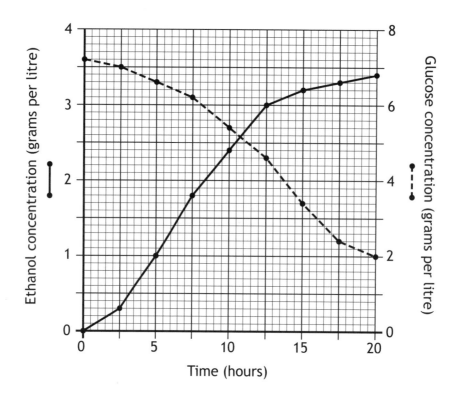

What was the glucose concentration when the ethanol concentration was 3·3 grams per litre?

A   1·2 grams per litre

B   2·2 grams per litre

C   2·4 grams per litre

D   6·6 grams per litre

8. The following statements describe stages in the Calvin Cycle (carbon fixation).

    1   Carbon dioxide attaches to ribulose bisphosphate (RuBP) producing 3-phosphoglycerate (3PG).

    2   3-phosphoglycerate (3PG) forms glyceraldehyde-3-phosphate (G3P).

    3   Glyceraldehyde-3-phosphate (G3P) regenerates ribulose bisphosphate (RuBP).

    Which row in the table identifies the stage which is catalysed by RuBisCO and the stage which requires hydrogen?

	Catalysed by RuBisCO	Requires hydrogen
A	1	2
B	1	3
C	3	1
D	3	2

[Turn over

9. The diagram shows apparatus used in an investigation to measure the rate of photosynthesis in *Elodea* (pondweed) at different wavelengths of light.

Coloured filters were used to change the wavelength of the light. The volume of oxygen collected after 30 minutes was used to measure the rate of photosynthesis.

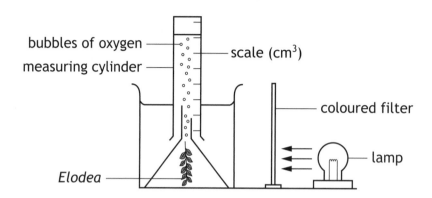

Suggested improvements to the investigation are shown.

1   Use a measuring cylinder with a narrower diameter.

2   Repeat the experiment several times and take averages.

3   Use a scale with more divisions.

Which of these suggestions would improve the accuracy of the results?

A   1 and 2 only

B   1 and 3 only

C   2 and 3 only

D   1, 2 and 3

10. The diagram shows a perennial weed found in agricultural land in Scotland.

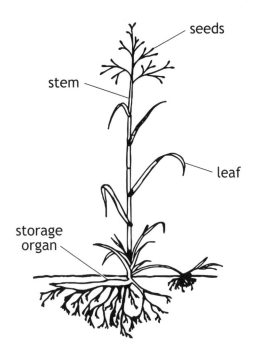

Which feature of this weed indicates that it should be controlled by a systemic herbicide?

A   Seeds

B   Stem

C   Storage organ

D   Leaf

[Turn over

11. A field trial was carried out to investigate the effect of mass of phosphate fertiliser applied on the growth of barley. The barley was planted in plots of equal area on a hillside and fertiliser applied as shown in the diagram.

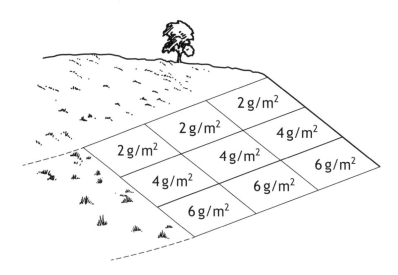

Which of the following procedures would improve the field trial design to take into account higher soil moisture levels at the bottom of the hill?

A   Increase the range of phosphate fertiliser masses applied.

B   Randomise the treatment plots.

C   Increase the number of plots.

D   Select another hillside.

12. Which of the following is an example of kin selection?

A   Worker leafcutter ants raising young ants in their colony.

B   A vampire bat regurgitating blood to feed an unrelated bat.

C   A dominant lion feeding on a zebra kill before its offspring.

D   A young orangutan spending a long period in parental care to learn complex social behaviours.

13. An experiment was carried out to investigate the growth rate of pigs. They were put into five groups of eight pigs, each with the same average initial body mass. Each group was fed a diet which contained either 0, 10%, 20%, 30% or 40% faba beans. The pigs were re-weighed each day for 40 days.

Which aspect of the experimental design increased reliability of the results?

A   Five groups of pigs were used.

B   The pigs were re-weighed each day for 40 days.

C   Each group had the same average initial body mass.

D   Each group contained eight pigs.

14. An investigation was carried out into the social hierarchy in a group of five hens, V, W, X, Y and Z. Hens establish dominance by pecking each other aggressively. The number of pecks given and received was recorded.

The results are shown in the table.

		Number of pecks given by each hen				
		V	W	X	Y	Z
Number of pecks received by each hen	V	—	—	—	10	—
	W	2	—	—	13	—
	X	6	8	—	7	—
	Y	—	—	—	.	—
	Z	11	10	5	4	—

The order of hierarchy from most dominant to least dominant hen is

A   Z, V, X, W, Y

B   Y, V, W, X, Z

C   Z, X, W, V, Y

D   Y, W, V, X, Z.

15. Each type of human cell has a different structure and function because

A   only some of their genes are expressed

B   they contain different genes

C   some genes are lost during differentiation

D   some genes are gained during differentiation.

[Turn over

16. The list describes some uses of stem cells.

1   Studying how cells differentiate

2   Researching the development of Parkinson's disease

3   Producing skin for skin grafts

4   Bone marrow transplants

Which of these uses are **not** therapeutic?

A   1 only

B   1 and 2 only

C   2 and 4 only

D   3 and 4 only

17. Which of the following is an example of sexual selection?

A   Koalas with resistance to disease surviving to reproduce.

B   Peppered moths with the most effective camouflage avoiding predation.

C   Plant breeders selecting barley cultivars to cross to improve grain yield.

D   Female black grouse mating with the male with the best display.

18. A population of finches became isolated on an island. The graph shows the range of beak sizes within the initial population at the time of isolation and in the population after many generations.

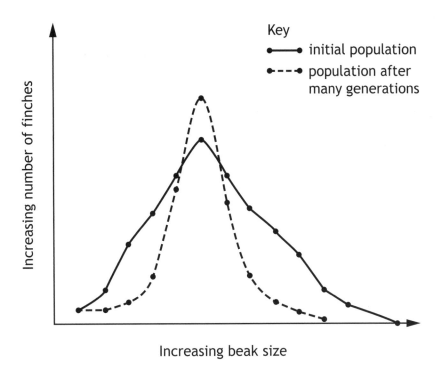

Which row in the table shows the type of selection pressure and the type of speciation which might be expected to occur in this example?

	Selection pressure	Speciation
A	directional	allopatric
B	directional	sympatric
C	stabilising	allopatric
D	stabilising	sympatric

[Turn over

19. Some processes involved in evolution are shown.

    1   sexual selection

    2   disruptive selection

    3   genetic drift

    Which of these processes involve non-random changes in the frequency of DNA sequences?

    A   1 and 2 only

    B   1 and 3 only

    C   2 and 3 only

    D   1, 2 and 3

20. The analysis of DNA sequences from different organisms is used in the production of molecular clocks.

    This analysis is based on the assumption that over time DNA sequences undergo mutations

    A   randomly

    B   spontaneously

    C   at a varying rate

    D   at a constant rate.

[END OF SECTION 1. NOW ATTEMPT THE QUESTIONS IN SECTION 2 OF YOUR QUESTION AND ANSWER BOOKLET.]

FOR OFFICIAL USE

National
Qualifications
2018

Mark

X707/76/01

Biology
Section 1 — Answer Grid
and Section 2

TUESDAY, 15 MAY

9:00 AM – 11:30 AM

Fill in these boxes and read what is printed below.

Full name of centre

Town

Forename(s)

Surname

Number of seat

Date of birth

Day   Month   Year

Scottish candidate number

Total marks — 100

SECTION 1 — 20 marks

Attempt ALL questions.

Instructions for the completion of Section 1 are given on *Page two*.

SECTION 2 — 80 marks

Attempt ALL questions.

Questions 11 and 14 contain a choice.

Write your answers clearly in the spaces provided in this booklet. Additional space for answers and rough work is provided at the end of this booklet. If you use this space you must clearly identify the question number you are attempting. Any rough work must be written in this booklet. Score through your rough work when you have written your final copy.

Use **blue** or **black** ink.

Before leaving the examination room you must give this booklet to the Invigilator; if you do not, you may lose all the marks for this paper.

SECTION 1 — 20 marks

The questions for Section 1 are contained in the question paper X707/76/02.

Read these and record your answers on the answer grid on *Page three*.

Use **blue** or **black** ink. Do NOT use gel pens or pencil.

1. The answer to each question is **either** A, B, C or D. Decide what your answer is, then fill in the appropriate bubble (see sample question below).

2. There is **only one correct** answer to each question.

3. Any rough working should be done on the additional space for answers and rough work at the end of this booklet.

Sample question

The thigh bone is called the

    A   humerus

    B   femur

    C   tibia

    D   fibula.

The correct answer is **B** — femur. The answer **B** bubble has been clearly filled in (see below).

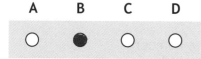

Changing an answer

If you decide to change your answer, cancel your first answer by putting a cross through it (see below) and fill in the answer you want. The answer below has been changed to **D**.

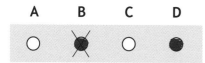

If you then decide to change back to an answer you have already scored out, put a tick (✓) to the **right** of the answer you want, as shown below:

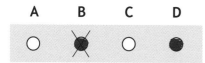

SECTION 1 — Answer Grid

	A	B	C	D
1	○	○	○	○
2	○	○	○	○
3	○	○	○	○
4	○	○	○	○
5	○	○	○	○
6	○	○	○	○
7	○	○	○	○
8	○	○	○	○
9	○	○	○	○
10	○	○	○	○
11	○	○	○	○
12	○	○	○	○
13	○	○	○	○
14	○	○	○	○
15	○	○	○	○
16	○	○	○	○
17	○	○	○	○
18	○	○	○	○
19	○	○	○	○
20	○	○	○	○

[BLANK PAGE]

DO NOT WRITE ON THIS PAGE

[Turn over for next question

DO NOT WRITE ON THIS PAGE

MARKS | DO NOT WRITE IN THIS MARGIN

SECTION 2 — 80 marks

Attempt ALL questions

Questions 11 and 14 contain a choice

1. The diagram illustrates thermoregulation in mammals following a decrease in body temperature.

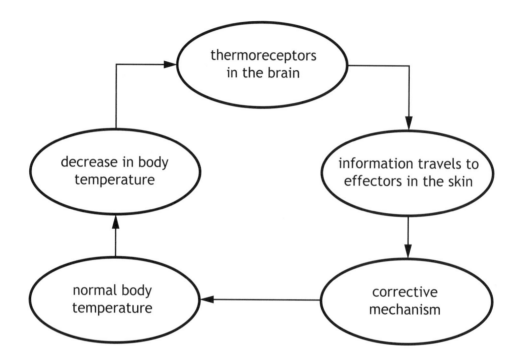

(a) (i) Name the type of control used in thermoregulation as shown in the diagram.   1

_____

(ii) Name the part of the brain in which thermoreceptors are found.   1

_____

(iii) State how information travels to the effectors in the skin.   1

_____

MARKS | DO NOT WRITE IN THIS MARGIN

1. **(continued)**

(b) Effectors in the skin include muscles in the walls of blood vessels.

(i) Describe the response of these effectors to a decrease in body temperature.

1

_____

_____

(ii) Explain how this response would help return body temperature to normal.

1

_____

_____

_____

(c) Explain why it is important for a mammal to regulate its body temperature.

1

_____

_____

[Turn over

MARKS | DO NOT WRITE IN THIS MARGIN

2. Daphnia (*Daphnia pulex*) is a species of water flea that lives in fresh water. An investigation was carried out into the effect of water temperature on the heart rate of one Daphnia. The results are shown in the table.

Water temperature (°C)	Heart rate (beats per minute)
2	175
7	184
12	194
17	207
22	219

(a) Calculate the average increase in heart rate per °C between 2 °C and 22 °C.   **1**

Space for calculation

_____ beats per minute per °C

(b) Daphnia is a conformer. Use evidence from the table to confirm this statement.   **1**

_____

_____

(c) Explain how an increased water temperature would result in a higher metabolic rate in Daphnia.   **2**

_____

_____

_____

(d) State the type of response shown by conformers to maintain an optimum metabolic rate.   **1**

_____

[Turn over for next question

DO NOT WRITE ON THIS PAGE

MARKS | DO NOT WRITE IN THIS MARGIN

3. The bacteria *Streptomyces* is a microorganism found in soil. It produces a secondary metabolite, the antibiotic streptomycin, which kills other microorganisms. *Streptomyces* live in close association with plant roots. These plants produce soluble carbohydrates which are released into the soil through their roots.

(a) (i) Name the growth phase during which streptomycin is produced. **1**

_____

(ii) Explain the advantage to *Streptomyces* of producing an antibiotic such as streptomycin. **1**

_____

_____

(b) The relationship between *Streptomyces* and the plant roots is described as mutualistic.

(i) Suggest the benefit to *Streptomyces*. **1**

_____

_____

_____

(ii) Suggest the benefit to the plant. **1**

_____

_____

_____

3. **(continued)**

(c) An investigation was set up to compare the effectiveness of streptomycin with other antibiotics by measuring the survival of bacteria. A species of bacteria was grown in the presence of different concentrations of antibiotics and the percentage which survived was calculated. The results are shown in the table.

Antibiotic	Concentration of antibiotic ($\mu g/cm^3$)	Survival of bacteria (%)
Fusidic acid	10	6
Chloramphenicol	25	42
Erythromycin	5	49
Gentamycin	10	5
Tetracycline	25	35
Streptomycin	10	35

(i) Name one antibiotic with which streptomycin could be validly compared.   **1**

_____

(ii) Give a conclusion which can be drawn from the results.   **1**

_____

_____

[Turn over

MARKS | DO NOT WRITE IN THIS MARGIN

4. The diagram shows information on the breeding and migration of Monarch butterflies (*Danaus plexippus*). Each generation dies after laying eggs.

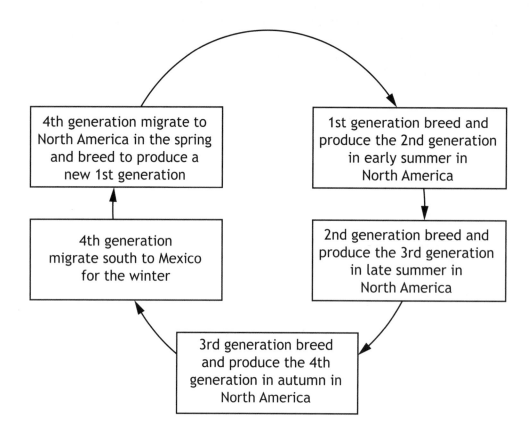

(a) State one advantage and one disadvantage to the Monarch butterfly of migration to Mexico.   2

Advantage _____

_____

Disadvantage _____

_____

MARKS | DO NOT WRITE IN THIS MARGIN

4.   (continued)

(b)   The migratory behaviour of the Monarch butterfly from North America to Mexico is innate.

Use the information given to justify this statement.   1

_____

_____

_____

(c)   Some species of hummingbird also migrate between North America and Mexico. They have high metabolic rates which they reduce while resting each night during the migration period.

Name this reduction in metabolic rate.   1

_____

[Turn over

5. The diagram shows some features of a plasmid which has been cut open by a restriction endonuclease to allow a gene from a donor chromosome to be inserted.

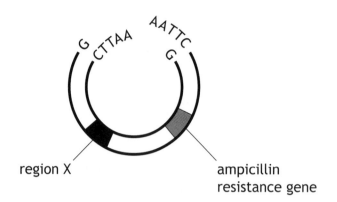

region X   ampicillin
                            resistance gene

The DNA recognition sites for three restriction endonucleases, *E coR1*, *BamH1*, and *HindIII*, are shown in the table. The arrows indicate where each restriction endonuclease cuts the DNA sequence.

Restriction endonuclease	DNA sequence recognised
E coR1	G A A T T C C T T A A G
BamH1	G G A T C C C C T A G G
HindIII	A A G C T T T T C G A A

MARKS | DO NOT WRITE IN THIS MARGIN

5. (continued)

(a) (i) A restriction endonuclease was used to remove a gene from a donor chromosome.

Use information from the diagram and the table to identify the restriction endonuclease which would be used to allow the gene to be inserted into the plasmid.

Give a reason for your answer.   2

Restriction endonuclease_____

Reason _____

_____

(ii) Name the enzyme which would be used to seal the gene into the plasmid.   1

_____

(iii) A culture of bacterial cells, 20% of which had taken up this modified plasmid, were grown on a nutrient agar plate. The plate was incubated and 250 colonies of this bacteria grew.

Predict the number of colonies which would have been expected to grow if the nutrient agar plate had contained the antibiotic ampicillin.   1

Space for calculation

_____

(b) Name region X, shown in the diagram, which ensured that the modified plasmid would be passed on to daughter cells.   1

_____

[Turn over

MARKS | DO NOT WRITE IN THIS MARGIN

6. An investigation was carried out to monitor the populations of red squirrels (*Sciurus vulgaris*) and grey squirrels (*Sciurus carolinensis*) in a 15 km^2 wooded area.

The average number of breeding pairs of each species was recorded between September 2010 and June 2012.

The results are shown in the graph.

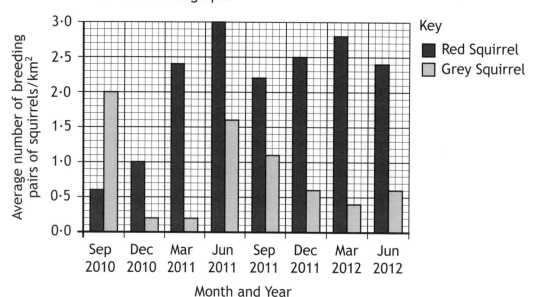

(a) (i) Use **values from the graph** to describe the changes in the average number of breeding pairs of grey squirrels from March 2011 to March 2012.

2

_____

_____

_____

_____

(ii) Calculate the **total** number of breeding pairs of red squirrels in the wooded area in September 2011.

1

Space for calculation

_____ breeding pairs

(iii) Express, as the simplest whole number ratio, the number of grey squirrels to red squirrels in June 2012.

1

Space for calculation

_____ : _____
grey   red

MARKS | DO NOT WRITE IN THIS MARGIN

6.   (continued)

(b)   Pine martens (*Martes martes*) live in wooded areas and prey on squirrels.

Populations of pine martens, red squirrels and grey squirrels were estimated in two other wooded areas using automatic cameras. These cameras are triggered by the movement of passing animals.

The results are shown in the table.

Wooded area	Estimated number of grey squirrels	Estimated number of red squirrels	Estimated number of pine martens
1	88	645	45
2	465	112	12

(i)   Suggest why the method used to estimate the numbers of pine martens and squirrels may lead to inaccurate results.   1

(ii)   Use evidence from the table which could be used to support the following statements.

1   Pine martens are more successful predators of grey squirrels than of red squirrels.   1

2   Grey squirrels compete more successfully for food than red squirrels.   1

(c)   Grey squirrels have spread rapidly and eliminated native red squirrels from much of the UK.

State the term used to describe grey squirrels in the UK as a result of this.   1

[Turn over

MARKS | DO NOT WRITE IN THIS MARGIN

7. Oil extracted from the seeds of the crop false flax (*Camelina sativa*) can be used as fuel. An investigation was carried out into the effect of a plant growth regulator paclobutrazol (PBZ) on the photosynthetic pigment content of the leaves and the oil yield from the seeds of false flax. The results are shown in the table.

Treatment	Average photosynthetic pigment content (mg/g of leaf)		Average oil yield (g/plant)
	Chlorophyll a and b	Carotenoids	
Untreated	3·28	3·02	1·7
Treated with PBZ	3·27	3·98	2·4

Absorption spectra for pigments from the treated and untreated plants were produced and are shown in the graph.

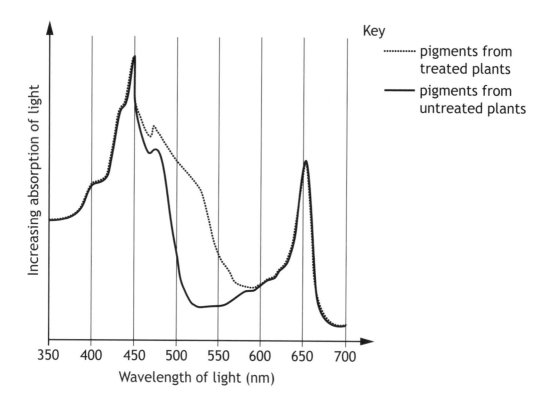

Key
.... pigments from treated plants
——— pigments from untreated plants

(a) (i) **Use values from the graph** to describe the difference in absorption spectra of the pigments from treated and untreated plants. 1

_____

_____

_____

MARKS | DO NOT WRITE IN THIS MARGIN

7. (a) (continued)

(ii) **Use evidence from the table** to explain the difference in the absorption spectra.

1

_____

_____

(iii) State one use that plants make of the light energy absorbed by pigments during photosynthesis.

1

_____

_____

(b) Suggest why seeds from the plants treated with PBZ yield more oil.

2

_____

_____

_____

_____

[Turn over

MARKS | DO NOT WRITE IN THIS MARGIN

8. Salmon can be reared in fish farms where they are sometimes fed small fish such as anchovies. Anchovies feed on animal plankton which feed on plant plankton.

The energy contents at each trophic level in this food chain are shown on a log scale in the bar graph.

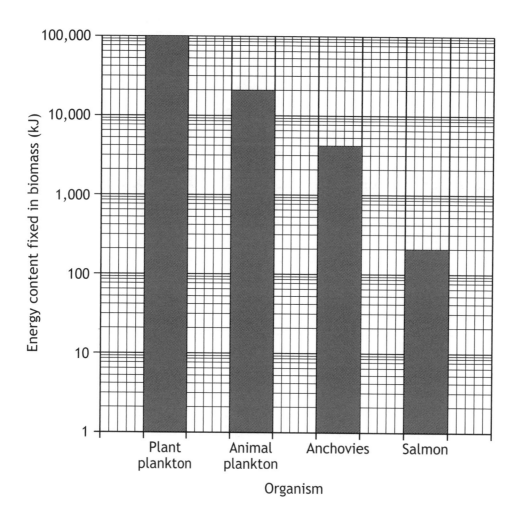

(a) (i) State the energy content fixed in the biomass of salmon. 1

_____ kJ

(ii) Plant plankton fix 2% of the solar energy they receive in their biomass.

Calculate the **total** solar energy to which the plant plankton were exposed. 1

Space for calculation

_____ kJ

MARKS | DO NOT WRITE IN THIS MARGIN

8.   (continued)

(b) The human population is increasing.

(i)   State the term used to define the ability of the human population to access food of sufficient quantity.

1

_____

(ii) In terms of energy explain the advantage to the human population of consuming anchovies rather than salmon.

1

_____

_____

_____

[Turn over

MARKS | DO NOT WRITE IN THIS MARGIN

9. The diagram shows crosses in a breeding programme involving different breeds of sheep.

(P)   Scottish Blackface female   X   Border Leicester male

↓

Greyface female (F$_1$)   X   Suffolk male

↓

(F$_2$)   Commercial lambs

(a) Suggest a reason why breeding programmes such as this include crossbreeding.

1

_____

_____

(b) Explain why Greyface sheep are produced by crossbreeding Scottish Blackfaces with Border Leicesters instead of breeding F$_1$ Greyface sheep together.

1

_____

_____

(c) To produce commercial lambs which show a desired dominant characteristic, Suffolk males homozygous for that characteristic are used.

(i) Name the type of cross used to identify if the genotype of the desired characteristic in Suffolk males is homozygous.

1

_____

(ii) Explain the importance of selecting a Suffolk male homozygous for the desired dominant characteristic.

1

_____

_____

MARKS | DO NOT WRITE IN THIS MARGIN

9. (continued)

(d) Spider lamb syndrome is a hereditary condition in sheep caused by a recessive deleterious allele which results in limb deformities.

State why inbreeding could cause an increase in the number of lambs born with this condition.

1

_____

_____

[Turn over

MARKS | DO NOT WRITE IN THIS MARGIN

10. An experiment was carried out to investigate the evolutionary relatedness of four species of fish by comparing proteins extracted from the fish. The more closely related species are, the more proteins they have in common.

A sample of muscle tissue from each species of fish was heated in a solution to extract proteins.

The protein extracts were analysed by gel electrophoresis which separates proteins according to their mass. A protein standard containing proteins of known masses was also analysed.

The results of the gel electrophoresis are shown in the diagram. Each band represents a protein.

Mass of protein in protein standard (kDa)	Distance travelled (mm)
16	50
20	38
26	30
44	24
66	15
108	10

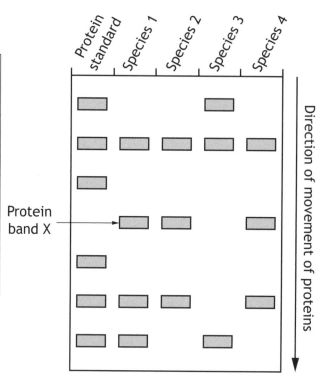

(a) (i) Identify **two** variables related to the protein extraction, not already mentioned, which should be kept constant so that a valid conclusion can be drawn.   **2**

1 _____

2 _____

(ii) During the preparation the samples were heated. This unfolds the proteins changing their three-dimensional shape.

Name one type of bond that could have been broken to cause this change.   **1**

_____

MARKS | DO NOT WRITE IN THIS MARGIN

10.　(continued)

(b)　(i)　Draw a line graph to show the distance travelled by the protein bands in the gel against the mass of protein in the protein standard.　**2**

(Additional graph paper, if required, can be found on *Page thirty-three*.)

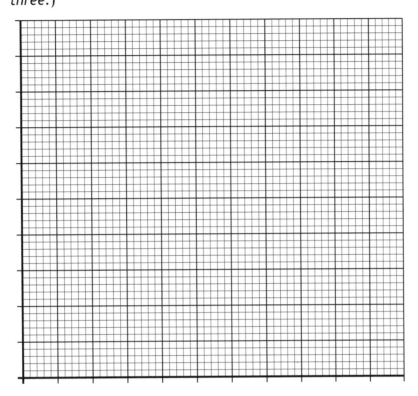

Mass of protein in protein standard (kDa)

(ii)　Band X travelled 28 mm. Use the graph to identify the mass of the protein in band X.　**1**

_____ kDa

(iii)　Each species of fish contains a protein with a mass of 66 kDa. One amino acid has an average mass of 0·12 kDa.

Calculate how many amino acids that would be expected in this protein.　**1**

Space for calculation

_____

(iv)　Explain why it was concluded that species 1, 2 and 4 are more closely related to each other than they are to species 3.　**1**

_____

_____

MARKS | DO NOT WRITE IN THIS MARGIN

11. Answer **either** A or B.

A   Write notes on components of biodiversity and how these are measured.   **4**

OR

B   Write notes on parasitic relationships and transmission of parasites.   **4**

MARKS | DO NOT WRITE IN THIS MARGIN

12. Congenital lactase deficiency in humans is caused by very low activity of the enzyme lactase, resulting in individuals being unable to digest lactose in milk. This is caused by a number of different mutations in the lactase gene.

(a) One of the mutations involved causes a frame-shift mutation in the lactase gene.

(i) Name a gene mutation which causes a frame-shift.   1

_____

(ii) Describe the effect of this frame-shift mutation on the lactase gene and on the structure of lactase.   2

Effect on lactase gene_____

_____

_____

Effect on structure of lactase_____

_____

_____

(b) (i) Some mutations occur in the sequences which regulate the transcription of the lactase gene.

Suggest why this may lead to more lactase enzyme being produced.   1

_____

_____

_____

(ii) Mutations in this gene are more common in Finland than in other parts of Europe. This is thought to be due to a small number of individuals who settled in Finland many generations ago.

State the term which describes this change in gene frequency when a small population of individuals breaks away from a larger population.   1

_____

[Turn over

MARKS | DO NOT WRITE IN THIS MARGIN

13. Scientists have used chemicals to produce polyploids to try to improve the characteristics of kiwi fruit plants.

The table shows some characteristics of fruit from the original diploid plant (2n) and two polyploids produced from it (4n and 6n).

Ploidy	Characteristics of fruit			
	Average fruit mass (g)	Average fruit length (mm)	Average fruit diameter (mm)	Vitamin C content (units)
2n	96·5	74·4	51·7	123·0
4n	115·8	76·1	60·0	119·0
6n	145·0	86·8	60·0	124·0

(a) (i) State which characteristic is least affected by polyploidy. 1

_____

(ii) Describe the relationship between ploidy and average fruit diameter. 2

_____

_____

_____

(b) Calculate the percentage increase in average fruit mass when the chromosome number is doubled. 1

Space for calculation

_____ %

MARKS | DO NOT WRITE IN THIS MARGIN

13.   (continued)

(c)   Describe the event that has occurred in the cells of the kiwi fruit plant that resulted in polyploidy.   **1**

_____

_____

(d)   Polyploids have whole genome duplications.

Explain the importance of this in evolution.   **1**

_____

_____

[Turn over

MARKS DO NOT WRITE IN THIS MARGIN

14. Answer **either** A or B in the space below and on *Pages thirty-one* and *thirty-two*.

    A   Write notes on DNA under the following headings.

        (i)   Organisation of DNA in prokaryotic and eukaryotic cells;   **4**

        (ii) The polymerase chain reaction (PCR).   **5**

    OR

    B   Write notes on RNA under the following headings.

        (i)   Structure and functions of different types of RNA;   **6**

        (ii) RNA splicing.   **3**

MARKS | DO NOT WRITE IN THIS MARGIN

SPACE FOR ANSWERS

MARKS | DO NOT WRITE IN THIS MARGIN

SPACE FOR ANSWERS

[END OF QUESTION PAPER]

MARKS | DO NOT WRITE IN THIS MARGIN

ADDITIONAL SPACE FOR ANSWERS AND ROUGH WORK

Additional graph paper for question 10 (b) (i)

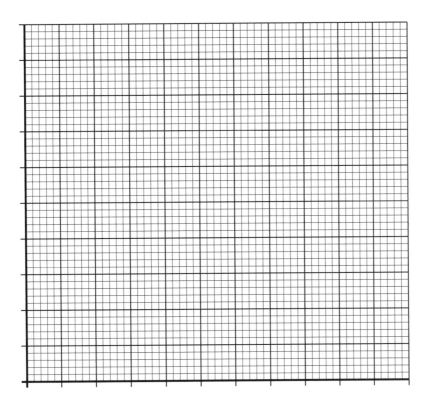

Mass of protein in protein standard (kDa)

MARKS | DO NOT WRITE IN THIS MARGIN

ADDITIONAL SPACE FOR ANSWERS AND ROUGH WORK

2018 Specimen Question Paper

National
Qualifications
SPECIMEN ONLY

S807/76/12

Biology
Paper 1 — Multiple choice

Date — Not applicable

Duration — 40 minutes

Total marks — 25

Attempt ALL questions.

You may use a calculator.

Instructions for the completion of Paper 1 are given on *Page two* of your answer booklet S807/76/02.

Record your answers on the answer grid on *Page three* of your answer booklet.

Space for rough work is provided at the end of this booklet.

Before leaving the examination room you must give your answer booklet to the Invigilator; if you do not, you may lose all the marks for this paper.

Total marks — 25

Attempt ALL questions

1. The genetic material in human mitochondria is arranged as

   A   linear chromosomes

   B   circular plasmids

   C   circular chromosomes

   D   inner membranes.

2. The main components of a ribosome are

   A   mRNA and tRNA

   B   rRNA and proteins

   C   mRNA and proteins

   D   rRNA and mRNA.

3. The diagram represents part of a protein molecule.

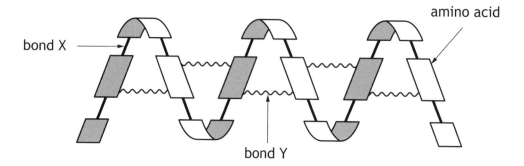

   Which row in the table identifies bonds X and Y?

	Bond X	Bond Y
A	hydrogen	peptide
B	hydrogen	hydrogen
C	peptide	hydrogen
D	peptide	peptide

4. Which row in the table describes research and therapeutic uses of stem cells?

	Research use	Therapeutic use
A	to repair damaged tissue	to study how diseases develop
B	to test drugs	to provide information on cell differentiation
C	to study how diseases develop	to repair damaged tissue
D	to provide information on cell differentiation	to test drugs

5. Types of single gene mutation are given in the list.

1   substitution

2   insertion

3   deletion

Which of these could affect only one amino acid in the polypeptide produced?

A   1 only

B   2 only

C   3 only

D   2 and 3 only

6. Which row in the table describes meristems?

	Found in	Type of cell present
A	animal	specialised
B	animal	unspecialised
C	plant	specialised
D	plant	unspecialised

[Turn over

7. The statements refer to DNA sequences in the chromosomes of eukaryotic species.

    1   code for protein

    2   regulate transcription

    3   are transcribed but not translated

    Which statements describe the DNA sequences which make up the genome?

    A   1 only

    B   1 and 2 only

    C   1 and 3 only

    D   1, 2 and 3

8. The table contains information about the relative genome sizes and number of genes found in a variety of organisms.

Organism	Size of genome (million base pairs)	Number of genes
Human	3080	30 000
Mouse	2600	25 307
Fruit fly	120	13 601
Yeast	12	6294
Mosquito	278	13 688
Nematode worm	97	19 873
Thale cress	125	25 000

    What conclusion can be drawn from the data in the table?

    A   The larger the genome, the fewer genes it contains.

    B   There is no relationship between genome size and number of genes.

    C   The larger the genome, the more genes it contains.

    D   The smaller the genome, the more genes it contains.

9. When comparing genomic sequence data, bioinformatics is the use of

    A   statistical analysis and fossil evidence

    B   fossil evidence and computer analysis

    C   computer analysis and pharmacogenetics

    D   computer analysis and statistical analysis.

10. Cell membranes contain pumps that actively transport substances.

Which of the following forms the major component of membrane pumps?

A Protein

B Phospholipid

C Nucleic acid

D Cellulose

11. The diagram shows how a molecule might be biosynthesised from building blocks in a metabolic pathway.

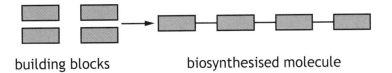

building blocks   biosynthesised molecule

Which row in the table describes the metabolic process shown in the diagram and the energy relationship involved in the reaction?

	Metabolic process	Energy relationship
A	anabolic	energy used
B	anabolic	energy released
C	catabolic	energy used
D	catabolic	energy released

12. An inhibitor of an enzyme-catalysed reaction can be described as competitive if

A its effect can be reversed by increasing substrate concentration

B it is the end-product in a metabolic pathway

C it prevents the gene encoding the enzyme from being switched on

D it changes the shape of the active site.

[Turn over

13. The stages of an enzyme-catalysed metabolic pathway are shown.

metabolite A

enzyme 1

metabolite B

enzyme 2

metabolite C

enzyme 3

metabolite D

In feedback inhibition

A   enzyme 3 binds with enzyme 1

B   enzyme 3 binds with metabolite A

C   metabolite D binds with enzyme 1

D   metabolite D binds with metabolite A.

14. The graph shows changes in the α-amylase concentration and the starch content of a barley grain during early growth and development.

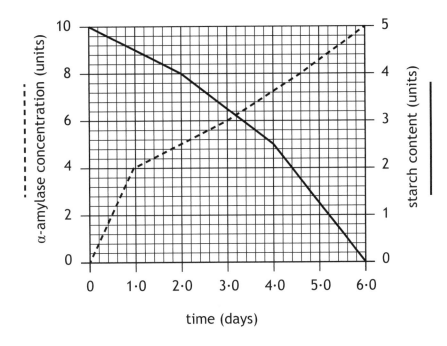

Identify the time by which the starch content of the barley grains had decreased by 50%.

A   2·0 days

B   3·2 days

C   4·0 days

D   6·0 days

15. Which of the statements describes a behaviour used to avoid adverse conditions?

A   Ruby throated hummingbirds enter a state of torpor every night.

B   Humpback whales swim from Alaska to Hawaii prior to the onset of winter.

C   European hedgehogs reduce their metabolic rate as a result of low temperatures.

D   Mugger crocodiles become dormant due to drought conditions.

[Turn over

16. The graph shows the effect of different concentrations of a disinfectant on the number of viable bacteria in liquid culture.

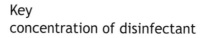

Key
concentration of disinfectant

● ———————— ● 5%
● - - - - - - - ● 10%
● —·——·—·— ● 20%

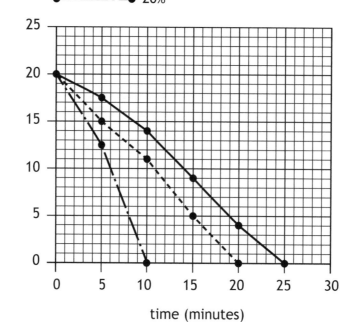

time (minutes)

What percentage of bacteria was killed by 20% concentration of disinfectant after 5 minutes?

A   25

B   37·5

C   62·5

D   75

17. The diagram shows a bacterial cell that has been magnified 800 times.

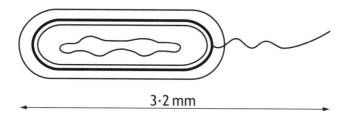

3·2 mm

The length of the cell in micrometres (μm) is

A   0·004

B   0·04

C   0·4

D   4·0

18. In which of the following domains of life are microorganisms found?

   A   Bacteria only

   B   Archaea only

   C   Bacteria and archaea only

   D   Bacteria, archaea and eukaryotes

19. A field trial was set up to investigate the effect of mass of fertiliser applied and the application of fungicide on growth of barley.

   The diagram shows the distribution of plots in the field and the treatments applied.

30	30	50
30	10	30
50	50	10
10	50	30
10	30	10
50	10	50

   Key

   ☐ Fungicide applied

   ▨ No fungicide applied

   10   10 kg fertiliser applied per hectare

   30   30 kg fertiliser applied per hectare

   50   50 kg fertiliser applied per hectare

   Which design feature was included to eliminate bias?

   A   Application of fungicide to half of the plots

   B   Randomisation of treatments

   C   Application of three different masses of fertiliser

   D   Use of three replicates

20. An action spectrum is a measure of the ability of a plant to

   A   absorb all wavelengths of light

   B   absorb light of different intensities

   C   use light to build up food

   D   use light of different wavelengths for photosynthesis.

[Turn over

21. The flow chart shows the energy flow in a field of potatoes during one year.

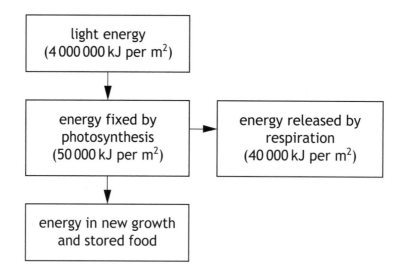

What is the percentage of the available light energy present in new growth and stored food in the potato crop?

A   0·25

B   1·00

C   1·25

D   2·25

22. The list describes observed behaviour of pigs on a farm.

    1   Stereotypic flicking of the head

    2   Repeated wounding of other pigs by biting

    3   Lying in a position which does not allow suckling

    Which of these behaviours indicate poor animal welfare?

    A   1 and 2 only

    B   1 and 3 only

    C   2 and 3 only

    D   1, 2 and 3

23. Adult beef tapeworms live in the intestine of humans. Segments of the adult worm are released in the faeces. Embryos that develop from them remain viable for five months. The embryos may be eaten by cattle and develop in their muscle tissue.

Which row in the table identifies the roles of the human, tapeworm embryo and cattle?

	Role		
	Human	**Tapeworm embryo**	**Cattle**
A	host	resistant stage	secondary host
B	host	vector	secondary host
C	secondary host	vector	host
D	secondary host	resistant stage	vector

24. The following statements describe symbiotic relationships between organisms.

1   Rhinos allow oxpecker birds to eat the parasitic ticks which live on their skin.

2   Spider crabs provide a habitat for algae which grow on them camouflaging the crabs from predators.

3   Female *Anopheles* mosquitoes feed on human blood from which they gain nutrients needed for the production of their eggs.

Which of these relationships can be described as mutualistic?

A   2 only

B   3 only

C   1 and 2 only

D   2 and 3 only

[Turn over

25. Ostriches are large birds that live on open plains in Africa. They divide their time between feeding on vegetation and raising their heads to look for predators.

The graphs show the results of a study on the effect of group size in ostriches on their behaviour.

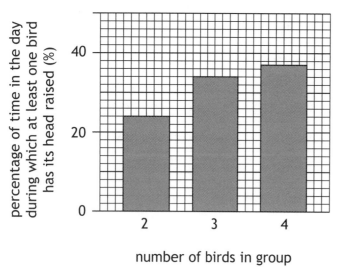

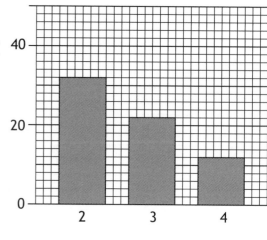

Which of the following is a valid conclusion from these results?

In larger groups, an individual ostrich spends

A less time with its head raised so the group is less likely to see predators

B less time with its head raised but the group is more likely to see predators

C more time with its head raised so the group is more likely to see predators

D more time with its head raised but the group is less likely to see predators.

[END OF SPECIMEN QUESTION PAPER]

SPACE FOR ROUGH WORK

SPACE FOR ROUGH WORK

SPACE FOR ROUGH WORK

H

Mark

National
Qualifications
SPECIMEN ONLY

S807/76/02

Biology
Paper 1 — Multiple choice
Answer booklet

Date — Not applicable

Duration — 40 minutes

Fill in these boxes and read what is printed below.

Full name of centre

Town

Forename(s)

Surname

Number of seat

Date of birth

Day	Month	Year

Scottish candidate number

Instructions for the completion of Paper 1 are given on *Page two*.

Record your answers on the answer grid on *Page three*.

You may use a calculator.

Use **blue** or **black** ink.

Before leaving the examination room you must give your answer booklet to the Invigilator; if you do not, you may lose all the marks for this paper.

Paper 1 — 25 marks

The questions for Paper 1 are contained in the question paper S807/76/12.

Read these and record your answers on the answer grid on *Page three*.

Use **blue** or **black** ink. Do NOT use gel pens or pencil.

1. The answer to each question is **either** A, B, C or D. Decide what your answer is, then fill in the appropriate bubble (see sample question below).

2. There is **only one correct** answer to each question.

3. Any rough working should be done on the space for rough work at the end of the question paper S807/76/12.

Sample question

The thigh bone is called the

    A   humerus

    B   femur

    C   tibia

    D   fibula.

The correct answer is **B** — femur. The answer **B** bubble has been clearly filled in (see below).

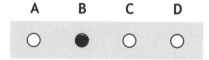

Changing an answer

If you decide to change your answer, cancel your first answer by putting a cross through it (see below) and fill in the answer you want. The answer below has been changed to **D**.

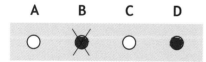

If you then decide to change back to an answer you have already scored out, put a tick (✓) to the **right** of the answer you want, as shown below:

Paper 1 — Answer grid

	A	B	C	D
1	○	○	○	○
2	○	○	○	○
3	○	○	○	○
4	○	○	○	○
5	○	○	○	○
6	○	○	○	○
7	○	○	○	○
8	○	○	○	○
9	○	○	○	○
10	○	○	○	○
11	○	○	○	○
12	○	○	○	○
13	○	○	○	○
14	○	○	○	○
15	○	○	○	○
16	○	○	○	○
17	○	○	○	○
18	○	○	○	○
19	○	○	○	○
20	○	○	○	○
21	○	○	○	○
22	○	○	○	○
23	○	○	○	○
24	○	○	○	○
25	○	○	○	○

[BLANK PAGE]

DO NOT WRITE ON THIS PAGE

H

National
Qualifications
SPECIMEN ONLY

Mark

S807/76/01

Biology
Paper 2

Date — Not applicable

Duration — 2 hours 20 minutes

Fill in these boxes and read what is printed below.

Full name of centre

Town

Forename(s)

Surname

Number of seat

Date of birth

Day   Month   Year

Scottish candidate number

Total marks — 95

Attempt ALL questions.

You may use a calculator.

Questions 9 and 17 contain a choice.

Write your answers clearly in the spaces provided in this booklet. Additional space for answers and rough work is provided at the end of this booklet. If you use this space you must clearly identify the question number you are attempting. Any rough work must be written in this booklet. Score through your rough work when you have written your final copy.

Use **blue** or **black** ink.

Before leaving the examination room you must give this booklet to the Invigilator; if you do not, you may lose all the marks for this paper.

MARKS | DO NOT WRITE IN THIS MARGIN

Total marks — 95

Attempt ALL questions

Questions 9 and 17 contain a choice.

1. The diagram shows stages in the production of three different proteins that are coded for by one gene.

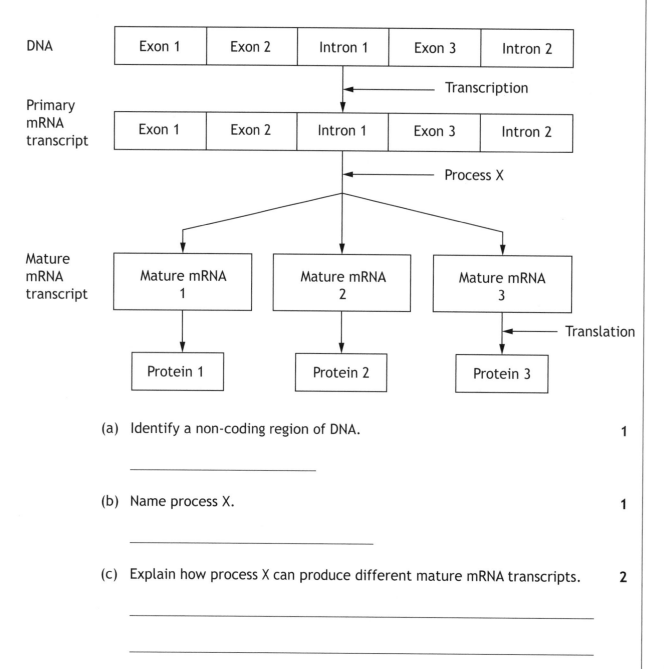

(a) Identify a non-coding region of DNA.   1

_____

(b) Name process X.   1

_____

(c) Explain how process X can produce different mature mRNA transcripts.   2

_____

_____

MARKS | DO NOT WRITE IN THIS MARGIN

2. A chromosome mutation in humans can result in the formation of the Philadelphia chromosome, which is associated with a form of leukaemia.

The stages leading to the formation of a Philadelphia chromosome are shown in the diagram.

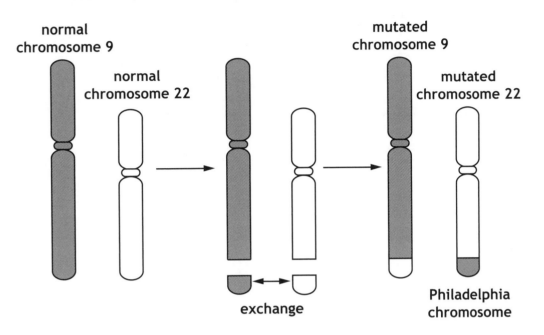

normal chromosome 9

normal chromosome 22

mutated chromosome 9

mutated chromosome 22

exchange

Philadelphia chromosome

(a) Name the type of chromosome mutation, shown in the diagram, which results in the formation of a Philadelphia chromosome.   1

_____

(b) (i) The presence of a Philadelphia chromosome causes a form of leukaemia through the over-production of an enzyme.

A drug has been used to successfully treat this form of leukaemia by binding at the active site of the enzyme.

Name the type of enzyme inhibition shown by this drug.   1

_____

[Turn over

Page three

MARKS | DO NOT WRITE IN THIS MARGIN

2. (b) (continued)

(ii) White blood cell counts in humans normally range from 5000 to 10 000 cells per μl of blood.

The table shows the white blood cell counts from a patient with leukaemia before and after treatment with this drug.

	Number of white blood cells (per μl blood)
Before treatment	150 000
After treatment	7500

Calculate the percentage decrease in the number of white blood cells after treatment with this drug.

Space for calculation

1

_____ %

(iii) Explain how the results suggest that the type of leukaemia in this patient was a result of the presence of a Philadelphia chromosome.

2

_____

_____

_____

3. The polymerase chain reaction (PCR) amplifies specific sequences of DNA.

   The flow chart shows how a sample of DNA was treated during a cycle of the PCR procedure.

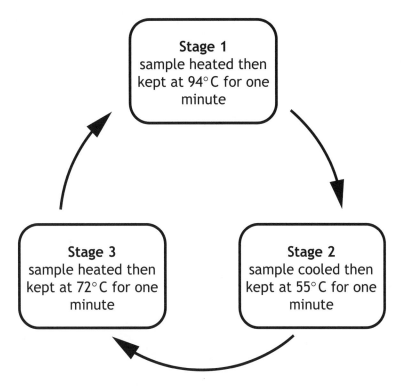

Stage 1
sample heated then kept at 94°C for one minute

Stage 3
sample heated then kept at 72°C for one minute

Stage 2
sample cooled then kept at 55°C for one minute

(a) Explain the purpose of the different heat treatments in Stage 1 and Stage 2.   **2**

   Stage 1 _____

   _____

   Stage 2 _____

   _____

[Turn over

MARKS | DO NOT WRITE IN THIS MARGIN

3. **(continued)**

(b) The number of DNA molecules doubles during each cycle of the PCR procedure.

Caculate the number of cycles needed to produce 128 copies of a single DNA molecule.

1

Space for calculation

_____cycles

(c) The diagram shows the contents of a tube used in PCR.

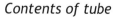
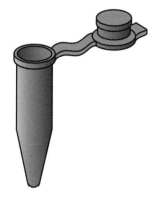

Contents of tube

— DNA
— DNA nucleotides
— primers
— enzyme and buffer

Describe the contents of a suitable control tube designed to show that primers are needed in the reaction.

1

_____

_____

(d) State **one** practical application of PCR.

1

_____

MARKS | DO NOT WRITE IN THIS MARGIN

4. The phylogenetic tree shows the evolutionary relationship between the three domains of life into which all present day living things can be divided.

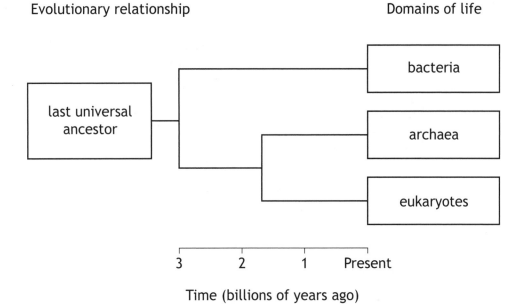

Evolutionary relationship   Domains of life

Time (billions of years ago)

(a) Name the type of data that can be used to confirm the evolutionary relationships between the domains of life shown in the phylogenetic tree.   1

_____

(b) Around one billion years ago genes were transferred between the prokaryotes archaea and bacteria.

Give the term that describes this form of gene transfer.   1

_____

[Turn over

MARKS | DO NOT WRITE IN THIS MARGIN

4. **(continued)**

(c) The phylogenetic tree illustrates the evolutionary relationships between primate groups.

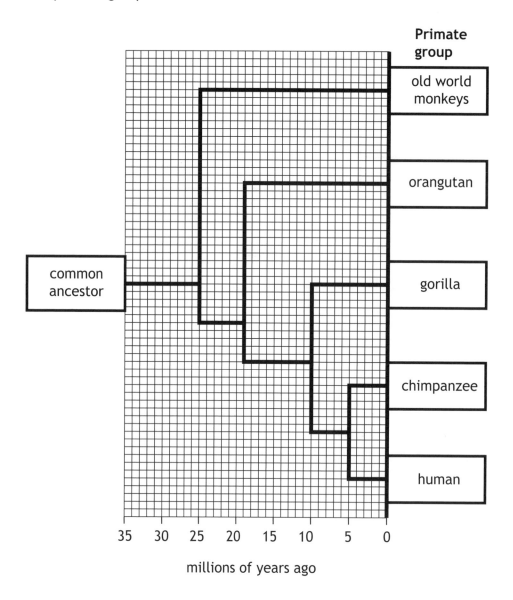

Primate group

millions of years ago

(i) State how long ago the last common ancestor of gorillas and old world monkeys existed.

1

_____ million years ago

MARKS | DO NOT WRITE IN THIS MARGIN

4. (c) (continued)

(ii) Humans are more closely related to chimpanzees than to orangutans.

Explain how this is known, using information from the phylogenetic tree.

1

_____

_____

_____

[Turn over

MARKS | DO NOT WRITE IN THIS MARGIN

5.   The diagram shows some stages in the aerobic respiration of glucose.

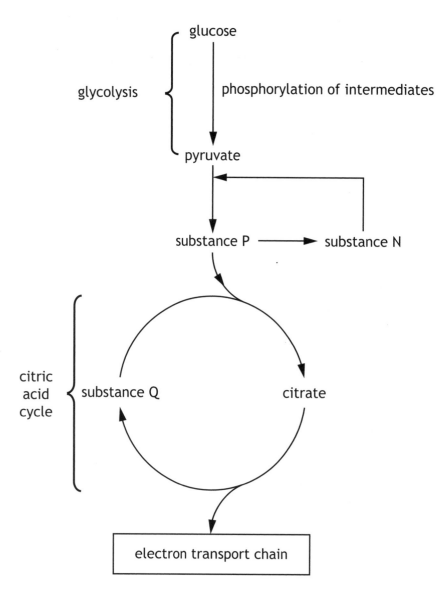

(a)   Name substances P and Q.   2

Substance P _____

Substance Q_____

(b)   Explain why the phosphorylation of intermediates in glycolysis is referred
to as an energy investment stage.   2

_____

_____

MARKS | DO NOT WRITE IN THIS MARGIN

5.   (continued)

(c)   Describe the role of the coenzyme NAD.   2

_____

_____

(d)   People who suffer from chronic fatigue syndrome have mitochondria in which some of the proteins embedded in the inner mitochondrial membrane are damaged.

Explain how this might result in the tiredness that is a feature of this condition.   2

_____

_____

_____

[Turn over

MARKS DO NOT WRITE IN THIS MARGIN

6. A growth curve in a culture of bacteria is shown in the diagram.

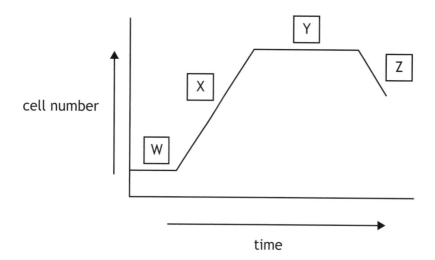

(a) In culturing bacteria it is important to control the culture conditions in the growth medium.

Name one condition which should be controlled. 1

_____

(b) (i) Name the phase in which secondary metabolites such as antibiotics are produced. 2

Describe the ecological advantage of this to bacteria in the wild.

Phase _____

Advantage _____

_____

(ii) State the letter which indicates a region of the graph in which most enzymes are being induced to metabolise the available substrate. 1

Letter_____

(iii) State **one** reason for the decrease in number of cells at phase Z. 1

_____

MARKS | DO NOT WRITE IN THIS MARGIN

7.   The graph shows the number of reported cases of hospital acquired infections (HAI) in one hospital between 2002 and 2008. The overall number of patients remained constant during this time.

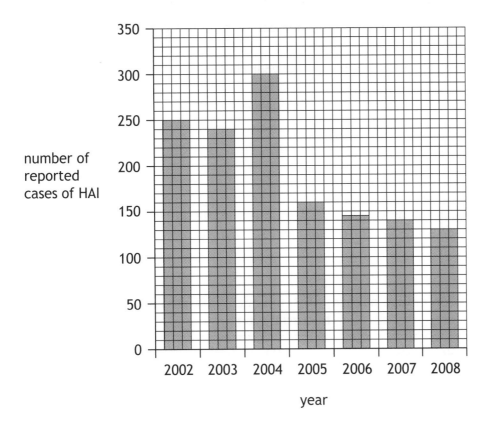

(a)   Using information from the graph, calculate the average decrease per year in reported cases of HAI between 2002 and 2008.

Space for calculation

1

_____ cases per year

[Turn over

MARKS | DO NOT WRITE IN THIS MARGIN

7. **(continued)**

(b) The decrease in the number of cases in 2005 was due to introduction of a new hand washing procedure at the hospital.

Predict what would happen to the number of reported cases of HAI in 2009.

Circle **one** answer and give a reason for your choice.   1

increase   decrease   no change

Reason _____

_____

(c) The table shows the percentage of cases of HAI in the hospital attributed to two types of bacteria, *Clostridium* and *Staphylococcus*, between 2002 and 2008.

Bacterial types	Percentage of cases of HAI in each year attributed to bacterial types						
	2002	2003	2004	2005	2006	2007	2008
Clostridium	32	30	30	51	54	57	59
Staphylococcus	34	32	33	30	31	33	33

Using information in the table, compare the overall trend in the percentage of *Clostridium* cases with that of *Staphylococcus* cases.   2

_____

_____

(d) **Using information from the graph and the table**, draw a conclusion about the effectiveness of the hand washing procedure against *Staphylococcus*. Justify your answer.   2

Conclusion _____

_____

Justification_____

_____

MARKS | DO NOT WRITE IN THIS MARGIN

7. (continued)

(e) Some bacteria form endospores to survive adverse conditions.

Identify which of the two types of bacteria in the table forms endospores and give a reason for your answer.

1

Bacterial type _____

Reason _____

_____

[Turn over

MARKS | DO NOT WRITE IN THIS MARGIN

8. Mammals are regulators and can control their internal environment.

(a) Give **one** reason why it is important for mammals to regulate their body temperature.

1

_____

_____

(b) (i) Name the temperature monitoring centre in the body of a mammal.

1

_____

(ii) State how messages are sent from the temperature monitoring centre to the skin.

1

_____

(c) The blood vessels in the skin of a mammal respond to a decrease in environmental temperature.

(i) Describe this response.

1

_____

(ii) Explain the effect of this response.

1

_____

MARKS | DO NOT WRITE IN THIS MARGIN

9. Attempt **either A or B**. Write your answer in the space below.

   A   Describe how animals survive adverse conditions.   4

   OR

   B   Describe recombinant DNA technology.   4

   You may use labelled diagrams where appropriate.

MARKS | DO NOT WRITE IN THIS MARGIN

10. Nettles are plants which often grow below trees. Their leaves contain photosynthetic pigments X and Y. The table shows the percentage of light of different wavelengths absorbed by these pigments.

Wavelength of light (nm)	Colour of light	Light absorbed (%)	
		Pigment X	Pigment Y
400	violet	40	20
440	blue	60	30
550	green	5	60
680	red	50	5

(a) State what else can happen to light striking the leaves of plants, apart from it being absorbed.

1

_____

(b) Identify which of the pigments in the table, X or Y, is chlorophyll a.

Explain your choice.

1

Pigment _____

Explanation _____

_____

(c) (i) Describe the relationship between the wavelength of light and the percentage of light absorbed by pigment Y.

2

_____

_____

(ii) Describe how the presence of pigment Y in their leaves would benefit nettle plants growing below trees.

1

_____

_____

_____

11. The average yield, fat and protein content of the milk from each of three breeds of dairy cattle were determined.

The results are shown in the table.

Breed	Average milk yield per cow (kg per day)	Average fat content of milk (%)	Average protein content of milk (%)
Pure bred Holstein	44·80	4·15	3·25
F_1 hybrid Holstein × Normande	48·64	4·25	3·10
F_1 hybrid Holstein × Scandinavian Red	51·52	4·25	3·15

(a) Calculate the percentage increase in average milk yield per cow from the F_1 hybrid Holstein × Scandinavian Red compared to pure bred Holstein cattle.   **1**

Space for calculation

_____ %

(b) The fat content of milk is important for butter production.

Calculate the total fat content in the milk produced in a day from a herd of 200 F_1 hybrid Holstein × Normande cattle.   **1**

Space for calculation

_____ kg per day

[Turn over

MARKS | DO NOT WRITE IN THIS MARGIN

11. (continued)

(c) Select **one** from: average milk yield per cow; average fat content of milk; or average protein content of milk.

For your choice, draw a conclusion about the effects of crossbreeding.   1

Choice _____

Conclusion _____

_____

(d) The development of pure breeds such as Holsteins has led to an accumulation of deleterious recessive alleles.

State the term that describes this.   1

_____

(e) Some F_2 offspring from crosses of F_1 hybrid Holstein × Scandinavian Red cattle will have less desirable milk-producing characteristics than their parents.

Give **one** reason for this.   1

_____

_____

12. An investigation was carried out to compare the rate of photosynthesis, at different light intensities, of green algal cells immobilised into gel beads.

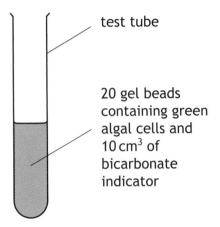

test tube

20 gel beads containing green algal cells and $10\,cm^3$ of bicarbonate indicator

Seven tubes were set up as shown in the diagram and each positioned at a different distance from a light source to alter the light intensity.

Photosynthesis causes the bicarbonate indicator solution to change colour.

After 60 minutes, the bicarbonate indicator solution was transferred from each tube to a colorimeter.

The higher the colorimeter reading, the higher the rate of photosynthesis that has occurred in the tube.

Results are shown in the table.

Tube	Distance of tube from light source (cm)	Colorimeter reading (units)
1	25	92
2	35	92
3	50	83
4	75	32
5	100	14
6	125	6
7	200	0

[Turn over

MARKS | DO NOT WRITE IN THIS MARGIN

12. **(continued)**

(a) Identify the dependent variable in this investigation. 1

_____

(b) Describe how the apparatus could be improved to ensure that temperature was kept constant. 1

_____

(c) Suggest why the tubes were left for 60 minutes before transferring the bicarbonate indicator solution to the colorimeter. 1

_____

_____

(d) Describe how the experimental procedure could be improved to increase the reliability of the results. 1

_____

_____

MARKS

12.   (continued)

(e)   On the grid, draw a line graph using the results in the table.   2

(Additional graph paper, if required, can be found on *Page thirty-three*.)

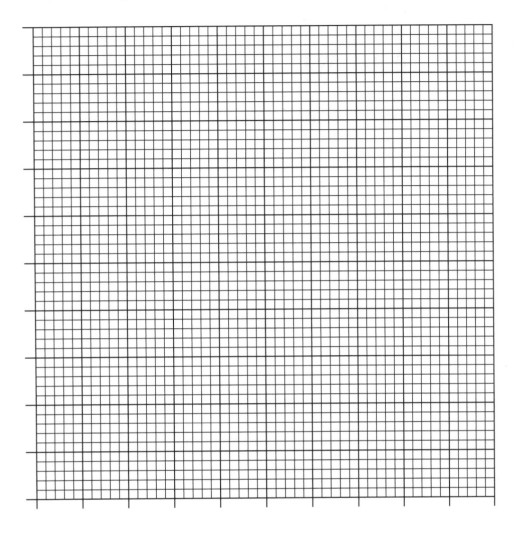

(f)   From the results of this investigation, draw a conclusion about the effect of light intensity on the rate of photosynthesis.   2

_____

_____

_____

[Turn over

MARKS | DO NOT WRITE IN THIS MARGIN

13. African couch grass is a weed which spreads rapidly from branching underground stems as shown in the diagram. If the plant's leaves are damaged, new leaves can grow from the underground stems.

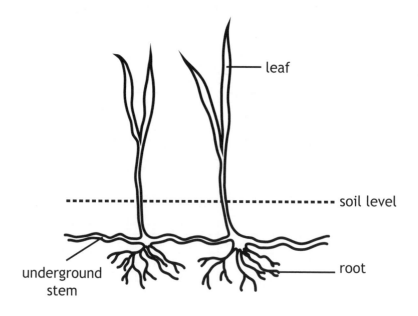

(a) State if this is a perennial or an annual weed and give a reason for your answer.

1

_____

_____

(b) (i) Explain why herbicide used in the control of this weed should be systemic.

1

_____

_____

(ii) Give **one** disadvantage of using chemical herbicide.

1

_____

_____

13.   **(continued)**

(c)   Explain why weeds are regarded as pests when they grow among crop plants.

2

_____

_____

_____

(d)   Herbicides are sometimes used along with ploughing to control weeds.

What name is given to this type of combined weed control?

1

_____

[Turn over

MARKS | DO NOT WRITE IN THIS MARGIN

14. (a) The honey bee (*Apis mellifera*) is a social insect that lives in colonies.

The queen is the only female in a colony that reproduces. Other females are workers that collect food, maintain the colony and care for the developing offspring.

Explain the advantage to the worker bees of caring for the offspring of the queen.

2

(b) The graph shows the changes in the number of honey bee hives kept by bee-keepers in the USA from 1945 to 2005.

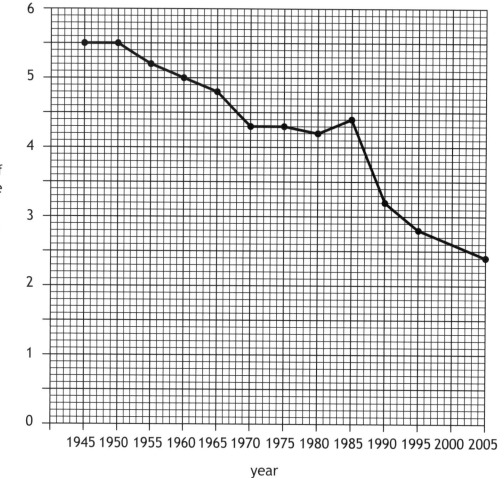

number of honey bee hives (millions)

year

MARKS | DO NOT WRITE IN THIS MARGIN

14. (b) (continued)

(i) **Using values from the graph**, describe changes in the number of bee hives from 1980 to 1995.

2

_____

_____

(ii) Calculate the simplest whole number ratio of the number of bee hives in 1965 and 2005.

1

Space for calculation

_____ hives in 1965 : _____ hives in 2005

[Turn over

MARKS | DO NOT WRITE IN THIS MARGIN

15. The genetic diversity of individual species is affected when fragments of woodland become isolated.

The diagram illustrates habitat fragmentation of an area of woodland over time.

The shaded areas represent woodland.

time

(a) (i) State what is meant by genetic diversity. 1

_____

(ii) Suggest a reason why a decrease in genetic diversity of an individual species can lead to local extinctions within habitat fragments. 1

_____

_____

(b) Explain how degradation at the edges of woodland habitat fragments affects biodiversity. 2

_____

_____

(c) Habitat corridors can be created to remedy habitat fragmentation.

(i) State what is meant by the term 'habitat corridor'. 1

_____

_____

(ii) Explain how a habitat corridor can increase biodiversity after local extinction. 1

_____

_____

MARKS | DO NOT WRITE IN THIS MARGIN

16. Japanese knotweed (*Fallopia japonica*) was introduced to Britain as an ornamental plant. It grows to 3 metres in height and has large leaves. It has become naturalised and has colonised many parts of the country where it out-competes native plants.

(a) Give the term used for a naturalised species that eliminates native species.

1

_____

(b) Name **one** resource for which Japanese knotweed may outcompete the native plants.

1

_____

(c) Japanese knotweed has spread very rapidly in Britain.

Suggest a reason for this.

1

_____

_____

(d) An insect from Japan, which feeds on Japanese knotweed, has been proposed as a biological control agent.

Describe **one** possible risk of introducing this insect into Britain.

1

_____

_____

[Turn over

MARKS | DO NOT WRITE IN THIS MARGIN

17. Attempt **either A or B**. Write your answer in the space below and on *Pages thirty-one* and *thirty-two*.

A Describe DNA under the following headings. 9

(i) Structure of DNA

(ii) Replication of DNA

OR

B Describe the evolution of new species under the following headings. 9

(i) Isolation and mutation

(ii) Selection

You may use labelled diagrams where appropriate.

SPACE FOR ANSWERS

MARKS DO NOT WRITE IN THIS MARGIN

SPACE FOR ANSWERS

[END OF SPECIMEN QUESTION PAPER]

ADDITIONAL SPACE FOR ANSWERS AND ROUGH WORK

ADDITIONAL GRAPH PAPER FOR QUESTION 12 (e)

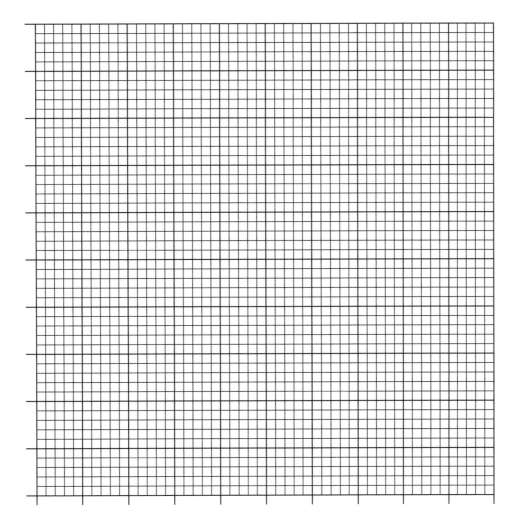

MARKS | DO NOT WRITE IN THIS MARGIN

ADDITIONAL SPACE FOR ANSWERS AND ROUGH WORK

Answers

SQA HIGHER BIOLOGY 2018

HIGHER BIOLOGY 2017

Section 1

Question	Answer	Mark
1.	A	1
2.	C	1
3.	C	1
4.	D	1
5.	A	1
6.	B	1
7.	B	1
8.	A	1
9.	A	1
10.	D	1
11.	C	1
12.	B	1
13.	D	1
14.	C	1
15.	D	1
16.	B	1
17.	D	1
18.	C	1
19.	B	1
20.	A	1

Section 2

Question			Expected answer(s)	Max mark
1.	(a)		Introns	1
	(b)		1,3,4/2,3,4	1
	(c)	(i)	Shorter protein/fewer amino acids. (1) <u>Stop</u> codon is produced earlier (in the sequence). (1)	2
		(ii)	Every amino acid after the mutation is changed/affected.	1

Question			Expected answer(s)	Max mark
2.	(a)	(i)	12	1
		(ii)	1.1 to 2	1
	(b)		Taq- Takes less time to amplify (sequence)/complete a cycle. OR Replicates/cycle/process faster. OR Cheaper as less heat is required/ temperature is lower. OR Taq takes 3 minutes and Pfu takes 4 minutes. OR Pfu- Proof reading/corrects errors.	1
	(c)		So it does not denature.	1
3.	(a)		From 2009/from the start it increases from 10% to 66% in 2015. OR Over the first 6 years it increases from 10% to 66%. (1) Then stays constant (until 2016). (1)	2
	(b)		Resistant plants survive. OR Non-resistant die. (1) Pass resistance- • genes/alleles/sequences • to next generation/to offspring/vertically. OR Reproduce/breed • and pass on resistance • genes/alleles/sequences. (1)	2
	(c)		Bacteria can exchange- • genetic material/plasmids • horizontally/in same generation • and charlock cannot/charlock transfers vertically. OR Horizontal gene transfer is faster (or converse).	1

Question			Expected answer(s)	Max mark
4.	(a)	(i)	Can only differentiate/specialise/change into a few types of cell/myoblasts/muscle cells/limited variety of cells/cells of the tissue that it came from (or converse).	1
		(ii)	Growth/repair/renewal of <u>muscle</u> (tissue). OR Increase number of muscle cells for growth/repair (of muscles). OR Become muscle cells for growth/repair (of muscles).	1
		(iii)	Does not involve destroying an embryo which some people believe is a human life.	1
	(b)		Testing/development of drugs/medicines. OR Study how diseases develop (or description of development of a named disease). OR Study cell growth/cell division/cell differentiation/gene regulation.	1
5.	(a)	(i)	550	1
		(ii)	260	1
		(iii)	Last common ancestor (of rats and humans) was more recent (than rats and frogs). OR Last/most recent common ancestor of rats and humans was 90 million years ago while rats and frogs was 420 million years ago. OR Rats diverged more recently from humans than from frogs.	1
	(b)	(i)	28	1
		(ii)	Any value from 27 to 28	1
	(c)		21	1
6.	(a)	(i)	Protein synthesis/translation/gene expression	1
		(ii)	1650	1
		(iii)	Microbes bacteria/other yeast/other cells may compete with yeast/use up nutrients/compete for resources. OR Microbes/bacteria/other yeast/other cells may reduce productivity/growth/yield of the culture/yeast. OR Microbes/bacteria/other yeast/other cells may cause disease/health risks/harm humans.	1
		(iv)	Add buffer/acid/alkali	1

Question			Expected answer(s)	Max mark
	(b)		A Phase — Lag (1) Description — Enzymes induced (1) OR B Phase — Stationary (1) Description — **(any 1 of the 3 below for 1 mark)** Culture becomes depleted of nutrients/substrates/resources/oxygen. OR Secondary metabolites produced/build up. OR Toxic metabolites/waste accumulate.	2
	(c)		Introduce genes/sequences that prevent survival (in external environment)/allow them to only survive in lab.	1
7.	(a)		Mitochondria are the site of (aerobic) respiration/electron transport chain/electron transfer chain/citric acid cycle, which produces ATP/releases/gives out energy. (1) Pumps/active transport/transporting salt requires ATP/energy. (1)	2
	(b)		So that enzymes are at their optimum activity/temperature. OR So that diffusion rates are optimum/high.	1
	(c)		Regulators have a wider/larger range of niche(s)/ecosystems/environments/habitats. OR Regulators have more niche(s)/ecosystems/environments/habitats. OR Conformers have a narrower/smaller range of niche(s)/ecosystems/environments/habitats). OR Conformers have fewer niche(s)/ecosystems/environments/habitats. OR Conformers have narrow niche(s) and regulators have wide niche(s).	1
8.	(a)	(i)	Time of exposure (to oxygen) Temperature Volume of blood Surface area of blood exposed Age of blood pH	1
		(ii)	40	1

Question			Expected answer(s)	Max mark
		(iii)	More haemoglobin is bound to oxygen at lower oxygen level/between 20 and 60 units. **OR** Haemoglobin is more likely to bind to oxygen at lower oxygen/between 20 and 60 units. **OR** They have 24% of haemoglobin bound to oxygen at 20 unit compared to 20 units/lowest oxygen. **OR** They have 70% of haemoglobin bound to oxygen compared to 50% at 40 units. **OR** They have 90% of haemoglobin bound to oxygen compared to 80% at 60 units.	1
	(b)		More red blood cells/EPO. **OR** Increased lung capacity/more capillaries/more alveoli. **OR** Increased myoglobin (in muscle cells).	1
	(c)		Description — Two atria and two ventricles **(1)** Explanation — Prevents oxygenated and deoxygenated <u>blood</u> mixing. **OR** No mixing of <u>blood</u> so only oxygenated blood is pumped round body. **OR** Oxygenated and deoxygenated <u>blood</u> kept separate. **(1)**	2
9.	(a)	(i)	Concentration of copper sulfate (solution)	1
		(ii)	Same experimental set up but with (same volume of) water in place of copper sulfate/0 mol l^{-1} copper sulfate. **OR** Full description of tube contents (10 cm^3 hydrogen peroxide, 5 cm^3 water/0 mol l^{-1} copper sulfate, paper disc soaked in catalase).	1
		(iii)	Water bath/incubator/oven	1
		(iv)	One disc/test tube/experiment used at each concentration/solution. **OR** Experiment was not repeated at each concentration.	1

Question			Expected answer(s)	Max mark
	(b)	(i)	Labels and scales correctly added. **(1)** Points plotted correctly and line drawn with ruler. **(1)**	2
		(ii)	150	1
	(c)		As the <u>concentration</u> of <u>copper</u> sulfate increased the activity of <u>catalase</u> decreased/inhibition of <u>catalase</u> increased. **OR** The activity of <u>catalase</u> decreased/inhibition of <u>catalase</u> increased as the <u>concentration</u> of <u>copper</u> <u>sulfate</u> increased.	1
10.	A		1. Have a social hierarchy which is a rank order. **OR** Have dominant/alpha AND subordinates. 2. Long period with parents/of parental care allows learning of complex/social behaviour/skills. 3. Ritualistic display AND appeasement behaviour occur. 4. Ritualistic/appeasement behaviour/display or correct example reduces conflict/tension/aggression. 5. Form alliances/grooming to raise social status/rank. 6. Behaviour influenced by ecological niche **OR** resource distribution **OR** taxonomic group. **(any 4)**	4
	B		1. Introduced (or appropriate description). 2. They become naturalised species when they are established (in the new area). 3. Spread rapidly. 4. May eliminate/kill off/destroy native/indigenous/original species. 5. Prey on/outcompete/hybridise with native/indigenous/original species. 6. Natural/original predators/parasites/pathogens/competitors are not present in new area. **(any 4)**	4

Question			Expected answer(s)	Max mark
11.	(a)	(i)	Transmitted/transmission. **OR** Reflection/reflected.	1
		(ii)	Excites <u>electrons</u> (in the pigment/molecule). **OR** Promotes <u>electrons</u> to a high(er) energy state. **OR** Produce high(er) energy <u>electrons</u>.	1
		(iii)	Broadens absorption/action spectrum. **OR** Absorbs more/wider range of wavelengths/colours (of light). **OR** Allows photosynthesis to happen over more/wider range of wavelength/colours (of light).	1
	(b)		(Photolysis of) water/H_2O	1
	(c)		Passes hydrogen to/reduces 3PG/3-phosphoglycerate. **OR** Passes hydrogen to form G3P/glyceraldehyde-3-phosphate. **OR** Reduces intermediate/compound to form G3P/glycealdehyde-3-phosphate.	1
12.	(a)	(i)	Reduced/no photosynthesis. **OR** Leaves are needed for photosynthesis. (1) Less energy/glucose/carbohydrate/respiration for growth. (1) **OR** Caterpillars are vectors for disease/spread disease to plants. (1) Disease reduces growth. (1)	2

Question			Expected answer(s)	Max mark
	(a)	(ii)	Chemicals — kill/harm other species/decrease biodiversity **OR** biomagnify/bioaccumulate **OR** accumulate/build up in organism/food chain/environment/ecosystem **OR** magnify up the food chain **OR** persist in the environment/ecosystem **OR** create resistant populations/pests **OR** on the crop can be harmful to health. (OR converse of any of the above written in terms of biological control/it) eg 'biological control/it does not kill other species'. **OR** Biological control only kills/targets caterpillars/one species.	1
	(b)	(i)	15	1
		(ii)	The original and modified Bt toxins used together kill more caterpillars than either alone. **OR** Modified Bt toxin kills 65(%) of caterpillars compared to 15(%) in Bt toxin but taken together they kill 80(%).	1
13.	(a)		14250	1
	(b)	(i)	Test (cross)	1
		(ii)	(Some/half would be) low gluten and (some/half would be) ultra low gluten.	1
	(c)		Deleterious/harmful/disadvantageous alleles would be eliminated/removed by natural selection.	1
	(d)	(i)	Number of grains	1
		(ii)	Cultivar — Sloop Justification — Starch content of grains is higher/highest (so may produce more sugar). Cultivar — ULG2 Justification — Amylase activity is higher/highest.	1

Question			Expected answer(s)	Max mark
14.	(a)	(i)	7	1
		(ii)	16	1
	(b)		They kill/catch/take down larger/more prey. OR Increased hunting success.	1
	(c)		Increases/ensures/allows the survival of shared genes/DNA. OR So that shared genes are passed on to the next generation.	1
15.	A		1. Occurs in the matrix of mitochondria. (1) 2. Pyruvate converted to acetyl (coenzyme A) losing CO_2. (1) 3. Acetyl (coenzyme A) combines with oxaloacetate to form citrate. (1) 4. Enzyme controlled. (1) 5. ATP is (re)generated/produced. (1) 6. CO_2 is released (during cycle). (1) 7. Dehydrogenases remove hydrogen (ions) and electrons. (1) 8. NAD/FAD becomes NADH/$FADH_2$. OR NAD/FAD is reduced. (1) 9. NAD/FAD transports hydrogen ions AND electrons to electron transport chain/electron transfer chain/inner mitochondrial membrane/cristae. (1) 10. Oxaloacetate is regenerated (or description of regenerated). (1) (any 7)	7

Question			Expected answer(s)	Max mark
	B		1. Animals survive adverse conditions/metabolic adversity by dormancy. OR All 3 types named (hibernation, aestivation and daily torpor). (1) 2. Dormancy is where metabolic rate/heart rate/breathing rate/body temperature is reduced. (1) 3. Dormancy/hibernation/aestivation/daily torpor conserves/saves energy. (1) 4. Predictive dormancy/hibernation occurs before the onset of adverse conditions (or correct description of adverse conditions). (1) 5. Consequential dormancy/hibernation/aestivation occurs after the onset of adverse conditions (or correct description of adverse conditions). (1) 6. Dormancy can be predictive or consequential (only award if neither 4 nor 5 not awarded). (1) 7. Hibernation occurs in times of low temperatures/winter/cold conditions AND aestivation occurs in times of drought/high temperature. (1) 8. Daily torpor occurs in animals with high metabolic rates. (1) **Max 5 marks from points 1–8** 9. Adverse conditions/metabolic adversity avoided by migration. (1) 10. Migration expends/needs energy/has a high metabolic cost. (1) 11. Migration is innate and/or learned (both terms required). (1) **Max 2 marks from points 9–11**	7

HIGHER BIOLOGY 2018

Section 1

Question	Answer	Mark
1.	B	1
2.	D	1
3.	A	1
4.	C	1
5.	D	1
6.	C	1
7.	C	1
8.	A	1
9.	B	1
10.	C	1
11.	B	1
12.	A	1
13.	D	1
14.	B	1
15.	A	1
16.	B	1
17.	D	1
18.	C	1
19.	A	1
20.	D	1

Section 2

Question			Expected response	Max mark
1.	(a)	(i)	Negative feedback (control)/homeostasis.	1
		(ii)	Hypothalamus.	1
		(iii)	Nerves/neurons/nerve impulses/electrical impulses.	1
	(b)	(i)	Blood vessels/arterioles narrow. **OR** Vasoconstriction. **OR** Muscles contract.	1
		(ii)	Less blood flow to the <u>skin</u> so less heat lost.	1
	(c)		So enzymes work fastest/faster. **OR** So enzymes are at their optimum (temperature). **OR** Enzymes work too slowly when temperature is too low. **OR** Optimal/faster diffusion rates.	1
2.	(a)		2·2	1
	(b)		As temperature increased heart rate increased.	1

Question			Expected response	Max mark
	(c)		Increased/optimum enzyme activity/oxygen delivery. **(1)** **Leading to** increased respiration/ATP production. **(1)** **OR** Increased diffusion **(1)** **Leading to** increased supply of oxygen/glucose/substrates/metabolites. **(1)**	2
	(d)		Behavioural.	1
3.	(a)	(i)	Stationary	1
		(ii)	Reduces/prevents/competition. **OR** Allows it to out-compete other bacteria/micro-organisms. **OR** Kills other bacteria/micro-organisms which might damage the plant thereby reducing *Streptomyces* food supply.	1
	(b)	(i)	The microorganisms can use/the carbohydrates for energy/food/respiration/nutrients/growth. **OR** They can feed on the carbohydrates.	1
		(ii)	The plant/it is protected from pathogens/diseases/bacteria/micro-organisms. **OR** Kills other bacteria/micro-organisms that might harm the plant/it.	1
	(c)	(i)	Fusidic acid/gentamycin.	1
		(ii)	Streptomycin is less effective than fusidic acid/gentamycin/others of the same concentration.	1
4.	(a)		Advantage — to avoid adverse conditions/metabolic adversity/lack of food. **OR** More food available. **(1)** Disadvantage — uses energy/metabolic cost. **(1)**	2
	(b)		Each generation dies after laying eggs. **OR** Only one/4th generation migrates.	1
	(c)		(Daily) torpor.	1
5.	(a)	(i)	Restriction endonuclease — EcoR1. **(1)** Reason — Complementary/same/matching sticky ends. **OR** Complementary bases/base pairs/DNA sequence. **(1)**	2

Question			Expected response	Max mark
		(ii)	(DNA) ligase.	1
		(iii)	50	1
	(b)		Origin of replication/replication origin/ORI.	1
6.	(a)	(i)	(The number of breeding pairs) rises/increases from 0·2 (breeding pairs)/km^2 in March 2011 to 1·6 in June 2011. (1) (The number of breeding pairs) then drops to 0·4 in March 2012. (1)	2
		(ii)	33	1
		(iii)	1:4	1
	(b)	(i)	The same animal may have been counted more than once. OR Not every animal passes a camera. OR Too few cameras/cameras only record animals in some parts of the area. OR Equipment failure or description.	1
		(ii)	1. When the pine marten/ predator number is high/ more/45 OR in wooded area 1. AND There are more red (squirrels) than grey (squirrels). (1) 2. When pine marten/predator numbers are low/less/12 OR in wooded area 2. AND There are more grey (squirrels) than red (squirrels). (1)	2
	(c)		Invasive (species).	1
7.	(a)	(i)	Treated plants have higher/ greater absorption (of light) between 450–600 (nm) or converse.	1
		(ii)	Treated plants have a higher carotenoid content/more carotenoid pigments.	1
		(iii)	Generate/converted to ATP. OR Produces hydrogen/H. OR Used for photolysis/to split water. OR Excite electrons/increase energy levels of electrons. OR Energy used to pump hydrogen ions across membrane.	1
	(b)		More photosynthesis. (1) More energy/glucose for growth/oil (production)/seed (production). (1)	2

Question			Expected response	Max mark
8.	(a)	(i)	200	1
		(ii)	5000000/5 million	1
	(b)	(i)	Food security	1
		(ii)	Less energy lost/more energy in anchovies as there are fewer/less trophic levels. OR Less energy in salmon as they are at a higher trophic level.	1
9.	(a)		Crossbreeds/F$_1$/offspring/ lambs may have improved characteristics/traits/genes. OR To get the best characteristics/ traits/genes from both (breeds). OR To introduce (new)/(desirable) characteristics/traits/genes. OR To produce hybrid vigour.	1
	(b)		Greater/increased (genetic) variation/variety (in F$_2$/offspring). OR Not all offspring will show desired characteristics.	1
	(c)	(i)	Test (cross)	1
		(ii)	All/higher chance of lambs/ F$_2$/offspring have (desired/ dominant) characteristic/allele/ dominant gene.	1
	(d)		(Inbreeding) results in the build-up/accumulation of (recessive/deleterious) homozygous alleles OR results in inbreeding depression	1
10.	(a)	(i)	Any TWO from: Size/mass/of muscle (tissue)/ sample. Type of muscle tissue/age of fish. Temperature/pH/time. Volume/concentration/type of solution.	2
		(ii)	Hydrogen/ionic/disulphide/ Van der Waals/hydrophobic/ covalent.	1
	(b)	(i)	Correct scales and label. (1) Correctly plotted. (1)	2
		(ii)	32 kDa or whatever plotted graph shows.	1
		(iii)	550	1

Question			Expected response	Max mark
		(iv)	1, 2 and 4 each have three bands/proteins in common/at the same distance **AND** 3 only has one band in common with the other three species. **OR** They/1, 2 and 4 have more bands/proteins in common/the same/similar or converse.	1
11.	A		1. (Measured) in terms of species, genetic and ecosystem diversity. **(any 2)** 2. A third example from point 1. 3. Species diversity is species richness and relative abundance/proportion of each species. 4. Species richness is the number of different species. 5. Genetic diversity is number and frequency of (different) alleles in a population/species. 6. Ecosystem diversity is the number of (distinct) ecosystems in an area/environment. **(any 4)**	4
	B		1. Parasite benefits/gains **AND** host is harmed/negatively affected. In terms of nutrients/energy/food. 2. Example of a parasitic relationship with parasite and host named **AND** benefit/harm described. 3. Parasites (often) have limited metabolism so cannot live out of contact with host. 4. Parasites transmitted/passed on by direct contact/resistant stages/vectors. **(any 2)** 5. A third example from point 4. 6. Some parasites have a secondary host to complete their life cycle or correct description. **(any 4)**	4
12.	(a)	(i)	Deletion/insertion	1
		(ii)	Effect on lactase gene: All the codons/base sequences nucleotide sequences/triplets/bases/nucleotides after the mutation will change/will move along. **(1)** Effect on structure of lactase: All the amino acids after the mutation may change **(1)**	2
	(b)	(i)	Gene is permanently switched on. **OR** More transcription occurred. **OR** Repressor molecule not produced so operator permanently switches on gene.	1

Question			Expected response	Max mark
		(ii)	Founder effect/genetic drift.	1
13.	(a)	(i)	Vitamin C (content).	1
		(ii)	From 2n to 4n (51.7-60)/above 2n it increases. **(1)** From 4n (to 6n)/above 4n it stays constant/levels out. **(1)** **OR** From 2 sets to 4 sets of chromosomes it increases. **(1)** Above 4 sets of chromosomes it stays constant/levels out. **(1)** **OR** Increases to 4n then stays constant/levels out. **(2)** **OR** It increases then levels out. **(1)**	2
	(b)		20	1
	(c)		(Complete) non-disjunction. **OR** Failure of chromosomes/chromatids to separate (at cell division). **OR** Spindle (fibre) failure. **OR** Errors during separation of chromosomes.	1
	(d)		Mutation can occur in extra chromosome/gene/DNA while original protein still produced/genes still function. **OR** Provides new/extra genetic material on which natural selection can work. **OR** Polyploid can no longer breed with the original population. **OR** Polyploidy can make (sterile) hybrids fertile.	1
14.	A	(i)	1. Prokaryotes have circular <u>chromosomes</u> and plasmids. 2. Yeast has plasmids. 3. Circular <u>chromosomes</u> in mitochondria/chloroplasts. 4. Linear <u>chromosomes</u> in nucleus of eukaryotes. 5. Prokaryotes have circular DNA **AND** eukaryotes have linear DNA (Only if point 1 or 4 not awarded). 6. Linear/eukaryotic/nuclear chromosome/DNA (tightly) coiled. 7. Linear/eukaryotic/nuclear chromosome/DNA packaged with/wrapped around proteins/histones. **(any 4)**	9

Question			Expected response	Max mark
		(ii)	a. Amplification/produces multiple copies of (target sequence of) DNA. b. (Heated to) 90°C–98°C to separate strands/denature DNA/break hydrogen bonds. c. (Cooled to) 50°C–65°C for primers to bind/anneal. d. Primers are complementary to/bind to target sequences/ DNA. e. (Heated to) 70°C–80°C so DNA polymerase replicates DNA/extends new DNA strand/adds nucleotides to new strand/3' end/primer. f. Heat tolerant DNA/Taq polymerase is used. g. Repeated cycles (of heating and cooling). h. Used in forensic/paternity etc. **(any 5)**	
	B	(i)	1. Single strand of nucleotides. 2. (nucleotide) contains ribose sugar, phosphate and base. 3. Adenine, cytosine, guanine and uracil. 4. mRNA takes copy of DNA code from nucleus to ribosome. 5. 3 bases on mRNA codes for an amino acid/is a codon. 6. tRNA picks up specific/one type of amino acid. 7. tRNA carries amino acid to a ribosome. 8. tRNA has anticodon AND an amino acid attachment site. 9. rRNA with protein forms a ribosome. 10. If points 4–9 not awarded, award point for stating mRNA, tRNA and rRNA. **(any 6)**	9
		(ii)	a. Introns removed from primary transcript. b. Exons joined/spliced together to produce mature transcript. c. Exons coding/expressed **AND** introns non coding/not expressed. d. Alternative (RNA)splicing produces different mature transcripts. e. (Different mature transcripts produced) depending on which (combinations of) exons are retained/spliced together/removed. **(any 3)**	

PAPER 1

Question	Response	Mark
1.	C	1
2.	B	1
3.	C	1
4.	C	1
5.	A	1
6.	D	1
7.	D	1
8.	B	1
9.	D	1
10.	A	1
11.	A	1
12.	A	1
13.	C	1
14.	C	1
15.	B	1
16.	B	1
17.	D	1
18.	D	1
19.	B	1
20.	D	1
21.	A	1
22.	D	1
23.	A	1
24.	C	1
25.	B	1

PAPER 2

Question			Expected response	Max mark
1.	(a)		Intron/Intron1/Intron 2	1
	(b)		(Alternative) RNA splicing	1
	(c)		Depending on which exons and introns are retained **(1)** different combinations of exons 1, 2 and 3 can be spliced together to produce different mRNA transcripts. **(1)** **OR** Appropriate example from diagram.	2
2.	(a)		Translocation	1
	(b)	(i)	Competitive	1
		(ii)	95	1

Question			Expected response	Max mark
		(iii)	Drug was effective as white blood count reduced to normal. **(1)** Drug works by inhibiting the enzyme produced by Philadelphia chromosome. **(1)**	2
3.	(a)		Stage 1-separates strands or breaks H bonds. **(1)** Stage 2-allows primer to bond/ anneal to strand/target sequence. **(1)**	2
	(b)		7	1
	(c)		Tube with same content but without primers.	1
	(d)		Forensic use/paternity testing/ diagnose genetic disorders.	1
4.	(a)		Sequence (data)	1
	(b)		Horizontal/lateral	1
	(c)	(i)	25	1
		(ii)	Last common ancestor of humans and chimpanzees was more recent than humans and orangutans.	1
5.	(a)		P is Acetyl CoA/Acetyl co-enzyme A. **(1)** Q is Oxaloacetate. **(1)**	2
	(b)		ATP/Energy is required. **(1)** A greater amount of energy/ATP is produced. **(1)**	2
	(c)		Carry hydrogen and electrons **(1)** to the electron transport chain. **(1)**	2
	(d)		Less ATP/energy is produced. **(1)** ATP synthase/carrier proteins damaged. **OR** Fewer hydrogen ions are pumped across the membrane/fewer electrons passed along electron transport chain. **(1)**	2
6.	(a)		Sterility/oxygen/temperature/ pH	1
	(b)	(i)	Phase – stationary **(1)** Advantage – allows them to out-compete other micro-organisms. **(1)**	2
		(ii)	W/Lag	1
		(iii)	(Cells are dying) because of toxic waste/secondary metabolites accumulating/building up/being produced. **OR** Running out/lack of/no nutrients/ oxygen/food/respiratory substrate. **OR** Increasing competition (for food).	1

Question			Expected response	Max mark
7.	(a)		20	1
	(b)		Increase — people becoming complacent about hand washing or bacteria becoming resistant. **OR** No change — everyone now using procedure. **OR** Decrease — increased uptake of procedure.	1
	(c)		*Clostridium* increases, **(1)** *Staphylococcus* remains fairly constant **(1)**	2
	(d)		Conclusion — effective **(1)** Justification — although percentage of cases remains similar number of cases falls. **(1)**	2
	(e)		Type — *Clostridium* Reason — percentage of cases due to *Clostridium* increased.	1
8.	(a)		So that enzymes are at their optimum temperature or for faster diffusion rates.	1
	(b)	(i)	Hypothalamus	1
		(ii)	Nerve impulse/electrical impulse through nerves.	1
	(c)	(i)	Vasoconstriction/vessels get narrower.	1
		(ii)	Reduces blood flow to skin so less heat loss.	1
9.	A		1. Metabolic rate reduced. 2. Dormancy can be predictive or consequential. 3. Hibernation in winter (usually mammals). 4. Aestivation allows survival in periods of drought or high temperature. 5. Daily torpor is reduced activity in animals with high metabolic rates. 6. Example of hibernation or aestivation or daily torpor. *Any 4 for 4 marks*	4
	B		1. Plant/animal gene transferred into micro-organism that makes plant/animal protein. 2. Restriction endonuclease to cut gene out/cut plasmid. 3. Genes introduced to prevent microbe surviving in external environment. 4. Ligase seals gene into plasmid. 5. Recombinant yeast cells to overcome polypeptides being incorrectly folded. 6. Regulatory sequences in plasmids/artificial chromosomes to control gene expression. *Any 4 for 4 marks*	4

Question			Expected response	Max mark
10.	(a)		Reflected OR Transmitted	1
	(b)		Pigment X **Explanation:** Absorbs in red and blue (light). Best/better/much more/mainly/ at a higher percentage/greater/ higher/more efficiently (than pigment Y/than green). OR Converse for green.	1
	(c)	(i)	As wavelength increases to 550 nm (percentage) absorption also increases (1) then decreases/as wavelength increases over 550 nm absorption decreases. (1)	2
		(ii)	Would allow absorption/use of light/green light/wavelengths/ colours. Not absorbed by/reflected from/ transmitted through/not used by/passing through/filtered through/transmitted by larger plants/the canopy/trees/sun plants/higher leaves/leaves above.	1
11.	(a)		15	1
	(b)		413·44	1
	(c)		Milk yield/fat content increased by crossbreeding. Protein content decreased by crossbreeding.	1
	(d)		Inbreeding depression.	1
	(e)		F_2 has a variety of genotypes.	1
12.	(a)		Rate of photosynthesis.	1
	(b)		Use a water bath.	1
	(c)		To allow time for photosynthesis/ for bicarbonate indicator to change colour.	1
	(d)		Repeat at distance/light intensity.	1
	(e)		Axes and labels. (1) Plotting and joined with a ruler. (1)	2
	(f)		As light intensity increases rate increases. (1) At higher light intensities rate remains constant. (1)	2
13.	(a)		Perennial **AND** can grow from underground stems.	1

Question			Expected response	Max mark
	(b)	(i)	Will kill/destroy the whole plant/ roots/underground stems **AND** so avoid regeneration/regrowth/ coming back.	1
		(ii)	May be toxic to animal species/ persist in the environment/ can bio accumulate/biomagnify in food chains/may produce resistant populations.	1
	(c)		Compete for water/nutrients/ light. (1) Reducing yield of crop. (1)	2
	(d)		Integrated pest control.	1
14.	(a)		Worker bees share genes with the queen's offspring. (1) So worker bees increase the survival chances of these genes by caring for the queen's young. (1)	2
	(b)	(i)	Increase from 4·2 million (in 1980) to 4·4 million (in 1985) (1) then decrease to 2·8 million (in 1995). (1)	2
		(ii)	2 : 1	1
15.	(a)	(i)	Number and frequency of alleles in a population.	1
		(ii)	Small populations may lose the genetic variation necessary to enable evolutionary responses to environmental change. OR The loss of genetic diversity can lead to inbreeding which results in poor reproductive rates.	1
	(b)		Increased competition. (1) Reduces biodiversity. (1)	2
	(c)	(i)	Area of natural habitat linking fragments.	1
		(ii)	Individual members of the locally extinct species can move into the fragment and recolonise fragments.	1
16.	(a)		Invasive	1
	(b)		Light/water/minerals/nutrients	1
	(c)		Free of pathogens/parasites/ competitors which were native to habitat.	1
	(d)		May eat native plants. OR May become invasive.	1

Question			Expected response	Max mark
17.	A	(i)	1. Double strand of nucleotides/double helix. 2. Deoxyribose sugar, phosphate and base. 3. **Sugar**-phosphate backbone. 4. Complementary bases pair or A-T and C-G. 5. Hydrogen bonds between bases. 6. Antiparallel structure. 7. Deoxyribose and phosphate at 3′ and 5′ ends. *Any 5 from points 1 to 7 for 5 marks.*	9
		(ii)	8. DNA unwinds. 9. Hydrogen bonds between strands break. 10. Primer needed to start replication. 11. DNA polymerase adds nucleotides to 3′ end of primer/3′ (deoxyribose) end of strand. 12. One strand replicated continuously, the other in fragments. 13. Fragments joined by ligase. *Any 4 from points 8 to 13 for 4 marks.*	

Question			Expected response	Max mark
	B	(i)	1. Isolation barriers prevent gene flow between populations/populations interbreeding. 2. Geographical isolation leads to allopatric speciation. 3. Behavioural isolation leads to sympatric speciation. 4. Ecological isolation leads to sympatric speciation. 5. Different mutations occur on each side of isolation barrier. 6. Some mutations may be favourable/provide selective advantage. *Any 4 from points 1 to 6 for 4 marks.*	9
		(ii)	7. Natural selection is non-random increase in frequency of genetic sequences that increase survival. 8. There are different selection pressures each side of the barrier. 9. Any 2 from disruptive/directional/stabilising selection. 10. Third type of selection from 9. 11. After many generations/long period of time. 12. New species form. 13. If populations can no longer interbreed to produce fertile young then different species. *Any 5 from points 7 to 13 for 5 marks.*	